GW01605846

OPERATION MIDNIGHT

Jonathan Kane Adventures:

FLY FOR THREE LIVES
OPERATION MIDNIGHT
LET THEM ALL STARVE (*in preparation*)

Jonathan
Kane

OPERATION MIDNIGHT

BY

Alexander Barrie
illustrated by Malcolm Hatton

FREDERICK MULLER

First published in Great Britain 1975 by
Frederick Muller Ltd., London NW2 6LE

Photoset, printed and bound
in Great Britain by
REDWOOD BURN LIMITED
Trowbridge & Esher

ISBN 0 584 63036 0

CONTENTS

chapter *page*

1 A Sniff of Action 1

2 Call the Tower and Go 26

3 Run—Get Out 49

4 Do Nothing Rash 76

5 Moment of Decision 88

6 You're on Your Own 112

7 We'll Put up Anything 135

8 We'll Try That. Pray 155

9 Company 191

For EMB

I must say "thank you" to my family for helping with this book, and to budding literary critics David Rafique and David Wood. I am also greatly indebted to the RAF—in particular to Flt/Lt Peter Britton, Wing Cmdr M. E. Bee AFC and Flt/Lt R. A. Cross for practical assistance. Finally, my thanks again to John Willis of Trans Europe Air Charters.

Chapter One

A SNIFF OF ACTION

"I'm having a lot of bad luck," said Jonathan Kane. "Unlucky, all the flipping time. Really I am. It doesn't seem right. It's just not fair."

He was sitting looking crumpled and dejected in the tower at Lonehead Field running a finger along the edge of an old desk, along and back again, and along and back again, feeling the slight roughness of the wood and allowing his mind to wander over the misfortunes of the past few days.

It was the second day of the summer holidays from school and in place of the blue skies he had hoped for were swirling stratus clouds as grey as his own thoughts.

Roz, more correctly Rosemary-Anne Hart, with the bright, good humoured, permanently slightly surprised looking eyes, was not so easily cast down. "It's not as bad as all that, Jon," she said cheerily. "I bet you've just forgotten the good things that happen."

"Nothing good has happened," replied Jon morosely. "These days nothing good ever does.

Remember last week my bike was stolen—I was in the shop hardly a minute and when I came out it was gone. Then yesterday I crashed my model aircraft, and apart from the fact that the plane itself is a write-off the radio equipment is badly damaged and that's expensive. Only single channel stuff but still expensive. And now, on my first day, the weather does this! You think I'm exaggerating, but I'm not. I really do have rotten luck." He stared out at Yankee Foxtrot, the old Aztec twin, standing forlorn and wet.

"Go on, don't make such a fuss," laughed Roz. "Your bike was insured and well, some boys of thirteen—all right, nearly fourteen—would think they were lucky just to be here, rain or no rain, helping Perry and Charlie run the airfield. And better weather is coming according to the forecast. So cheer up."

Peregrene Langhorne, owner of the field and of Western Aircharters, and Charlie Thompson, Chief Instructor of the Mid Country Flying Club were also in the tower but remained silent during this exchange. Perry was grappling with the paper work which always faced him and which he tackled with diligence if not great skill; brilliant pilot and navigator that he was, he made no pretence at being a scholar. "How d'you spell licensee?" he would ask Roz. And, "Roz, work out the fuel tax refund for the trip to Rome. I reckon it would be on seventy gallons. What does that come out to?" Obligingly, Roz came back with the answer every time. Roz was cool, efficient, beautiful; a dream girl and deeply stuck

NO SMOKING

on Perry.

The problem today was discounts. "If we pay the Engine Supplies account now, what d'you reckon we can knock off. Maybe ten?" Roz nodded. "Try ten," she said.

Perry grunted. "Sometimes I feel I'm just a goddammed flying clerk," he complained, but smiled briefly as he spoke. "I don't know what I'd do without you Rozzie, my sugar plum pie."

"I know," said Roz cheerfully. "I know exactly what you'd do."

Perry glanced up, on guard. "You do, eh?"

"Sure. You'd find another girl in five minutes flat. That's what you'd do."

The smile on Perry's lean, weathered face grew. "Jeeze, you're so wrong," he said. "I'd die in an hour from a broken heart."

Charlie pulled himself to his feet and wandered to the rain-drenched window. "I don't know what you all see in him," he muttered nodding vaguely towards Perry. "Beautiful women rush towards him like moths to a flame. And he can't even cook! Jonno boy, Captain, make us some coffee."

"Coffee? But it's only—oh, all right then. If you insist."

Jon was rising to reach for the coffee pot when the telephone rang beside him.

"Answer it, Jon," said Perry. "And do me a favour. Sound cheerful or we'll all be in tears."

Jon spoke for a moment or two, then turned to Perry. "It's for you. A call from London."

"Aw heck! Not now. Ask who it is and what he wants. Take his number and say I'll ring him back when I've finished this stupid bit of paper."

Jon passed the message politely, then paused, listening. "Just a minute, please," he said at last. "I'll tell Mr Langhorne." He turned once more to Perry. "It's the government. A man called Sir Hartley Peers. He says it's very urgent and he wants you to go to his office. He'd like you to come to the 'phone at once."

"Peers?" murmured Perry. "I remember him. I've flown him. The guy with the white carnation in his button hole and the pin-stripe trousers. Now what's itching him?" He picked up the telephone.

"Langhorne here," he said in the quiet, accented voice that still gave away traces of his early life in the southern states of America.

"Mr Langhorne, good morning. My name is Peers—ah, Sir Hartley. We've met before."

"Sure. I remember you."

"Splendid. I hope you are keeping well." Me keeping well? thought Perry. So what does he care? But of course Peers had always been one for the conversational pleasantries. *Toujours la politesse.* A few throw away sentences and then—wait for it, wait for it—zambang, the crunch.

"I'm fine."

"Delighted to hear it. Not much of a summer, is it? I wonder you don't go back to the sunshine of Florida, pluck the oranges off the trees and all that sort of thing." Perry paused, recollecting the voice, the impeccable, lightly pitched voice that had droned its quiet, relentless way through the best clubs and drawing rooms of Europe and New York. Peers always sounded soft, like a grown-up mother's boy full of whimsicality and foppishness but, as Perry well knew, the impression was most misleading. A mind as cold, quick and ruthless as a gin-trap lay behind the polished mannerisms of this man, a top civil servant, Private Secretary to the Secretary of State at the Foreign Office and trusted advisor to the Foreign Secretary, other members of the government and even to the Prime Minister himself. Indeed, where overseas interests were involved, the recommendations of Sir Hartley Peers, KCB, MC, and the official policy that followed were usually much the same. "I have no special skill, my dear chap," he had once said to Perry. "No crystal ball. I'm just very cerebral about life."

Cerebral? While Perry was still pondering the meaning of the expression Sir Hartley had obligingly explained. "You see, unlike most people, I *think*. I don't fog myself up with feelings. D'you follow? I just state the problems clearly and answers appear by themselves. A useful trick."

"It's actually some time since I saw an orange grove," said Perry drily. "Like maybe twenty years. What can I do for you, Sir Hartley?"

"I'd like you to call on me, here, in Whitehall."

"I'm pretty tied up for the next few days. What date d'you have in mind?"

To Peregrene's surprise Sir Hartley replied with a

little snatch of song, a wholly irrelevant snatch of song from *The Gondoliers* delivered in a reedy, off-tune hum. Then, after a pause, came the famous Peers crunch in one clipped word: "Today."

"Today? That's impossible."

"It's necessary. And, ah, likely to be profitable."

"Look, it's a long drive from Lonehead to London. A long drive and a wet day . . ."

"A ministry car is on its way to you, Mr Langhorne. I would expect it to be with you in, say, half an hour. Have the kindness to be in it when it returns. Good morning." During the second or so that it took Sir Hartley to hang up, more strains of *The Gondoliers* came, still as tunelessly, from the earpiece.

Perry turned to the others. "Well, whadyaknow," he said. "That guy has nerve. Man, does he have nerve! He wants me in London today and he's already sent a car."

Charlie brightened. "It's something to do," he said. I'll go along with you—I mean just for the ride. Is that okay?"

"Sure."

"And what about me? Can I come?" Jonathan looked hopeful.

"You, too. We can't leave you behind, Jonno." He turned to Rosemary-Anne. "Roz, will you, um . . .?"

"Yes, Perry, don't worry. I'll stay here and, now, what's the expression? Oh yes, 'look after the fort'. Have a nice time."

Perry winced. "Now don't be nasty, Roz. We'll

put you on the payroll someday. Promise." Then, genuinely concerned: "Will you be all right? Are you sure?"

She nodded agreeably. "I don't want to go to London in the rain."

"Where the heck is that coffee, Jon?" asked Perry changing the subject. "And when you've made it, I'd like to see Oscar X-Ray in the hangar—those split canopies aren't waterproof in rain like this as everybody here should know. I'll bet it's darned well half full of water. Put your waterproof drawers on, Jon, and taxi it into the hangar. That is if you can remember how."

Jonathan stood for one delighted, silent moment, then dashed from the room. "Make the coffee, Charlie," he said as he ran. "I'm putting Oscar X-Ray away."

He ran down the long flight of stairs that led from the so-called tower, the little operations room perched on the roof of the one hangar at Lonehead field, and out into the rain. Oscar X-Ray, the smart, French-built little three/four seater Knight was standing there dripping water like a shirt hung out to dry. Jon clambered onto the wing, opened the door and eased himself into the left hand seat, gritting his teeth as his bottom went down into the cold wetness of the cockpit. Perry had been right. Lots of water had come through the crack in the roof. But who cared? He was back in an aircraft again, after twelve long grinding weeks at school; and it was a particularly nice aircraft, and he had permission to start it up. Life was suddenly very good.

Like many pilots, Jon liked to talk to himself while carrying out his drills, and he did so now. "Brakes on," he said, noting that the pistol-type hand brake grip was pulled out and turned to the locked position. "Now, let's have the battery master on." He pushed the control knob on the dashboard fully in, watched the instrument needles flick up to show their readings and heard the quiet whine of the gyros begin; so the circuits were live. Good. "Now, fuel pump on," and he moved the switch upward; immediately the pump did its work, lifting petrol to the carburettor and clicking quite loudly while doing so. "Now, six priming strokes with the throttle"—and he pushed the throttle knob firmly in and out to charge the cylinders with fuel, leaving the control set carefully for fast tick-over, about a quarter open. "Now a look round." There was nobody near the propeller or slipstream so no reason to delay. "Right then, here we go." He turned the ignition switch to both mags "on" and, smiling broadly from the sheer delight of the thing, pressed the start button.

To the unmistakeable accompaniment of the chow-wow-wow sound an aero engine makes as it strains to start, the propeller began to turn, struggling and jerking as the pistons moved in and out of the compression cycle, and then suddenly it was away, roaring with power and making music that Jon wouldn't have changed for every symphony orchestra in the world—real though his interest in music had become.

Rain drops on the windscreen began to disperse now in jerky rivulets, pressed on by the slipstream. Visibility was fair—not good, but enough as the water cleared. Usually he sat on a plastic, inflatable cushion with another one stuffed behind the small of his back, but for this little taxying job he hadn't thought to bring them. He felt rather low in the seat and knew that full movement of the rudder bar would be beyond the twenty-nine inch reach of his leg. Even more than ordinary care would be required.

He released the brake and waited to see if the aircraft moved. The wheels were restrained by the long, wet grass and it didn't. Cautiously he put on more power. With fifteen hundred revs on the clock she began to roll and Jon, very pleased with himself, grinned more broadly than ever. He was totally happy. Maybe life wasn't entirely bad luck after all.

By the time he re-appeared in the tower he was wet from knees to waist and Roz looked him over disapprovingly. "Jon, you *are* a chump," she said. "You're all the same on this field—hopeless. You'll have to go and change. Go on, or you'll catch cold—and I'm not reckoning to nurse you." Jon sighed loudly; women, even nice ones, were all the same too: fussers.

The big black limousine splashed through the rain to the control tower at ten forty-five, and a few minutes later the three of them were on their way in VIP comfort. The chauffeur drove very fast and skilfully; Jon, sitting in front and securely belted in, watched with interest as the heavy car raced along the straights, took curves at speed without the hint of a slide, hammered through the rain and, finally, pushed into the crawling traffic of the capital to stop at last at the Foreign Office.

"I think you'd better come in with me, Charlie," suggested Perry. "I have the feeling I'd like a witness to the conversation. Come on."

But Charlie didn't want to go. His lips and ragged, reddish moustache moved into a melancholy, downward curve. "Not me, Perry," he said. "This isn't my kind of scene. Honestly. I'll just paddle through the rain—have a look at the town. Take the Captain."

"Yes, please," said Jon eagerly. "I'll come."

Perry hesitated for a moment, then nodded his head. "Okay. Let's go. Don't get lost, Charlie—and don't be away for more than half an hour or so. I want to be heading back to the field before long." Perry and Jon stepped from the car and hurried into the drab stone building of the Foreign Office. Inside, a commissionaire stopped them at once. "Can I help you?" he asked, but without looking as if he intended to.

"I guess so. Sir Hartley Peers is expecting me—us," said Perry, stretching the truth a little with the "us".

"Ah, indeed, sir." The man's expression changed for the better. "Sir Hartley himself. I see. If you'll report to the reception desk over there you'll be taken to him."

It would be difficult to say who was the more surprised, Perry or Jon, at the sight of Sir Hartley's office. The room was huge and luxurious, lined with well filled bookshelves, thickly carpeted and smelling in some indefinable way of leather and antiquity. Sir Hartley's desk was not a desk at all but a table big enough to use for a minor state banquet. As the two visitors stood quite still for a moment, taking it all in, the dapper figure of Sir Hartley moved smilingly towards them. "How kind of you to come, Mr Langhorne. I was relying on you. I hope you had a pleasant journey?" His hand was held out and Perry obligingly shook it.

"Quite pleasant, thanks."

Sir Hartley turned his cold, sharp eyes towards Jonathan and held out the smallish white hand again. "And who is this young man?"

"Oh, that's Jon. Jonathan Kane. He spends most of his school holidays with us at Lonehead. He's one of the crew these days."

"How pleasant. What a novel idea." Sir Hartley beamed. "Now, Jonathan, I would prefer to speak to Mr Langhorne alone so I'll have you escorted to the waiting room. There are books and magazines you can read there. We shouldn't be frightfully long." He began reaching towards a bell-push in the wall.

"One moment, Sir Hartley. Don't press the bell." Perry's lips were looking thin and straight. "I'd prefer Jonathan to stay here, with us."

Sir Hartley's beam increased and he reached for the internal telephone. "Smedley," he said after a moment into the voicepiece, "d'you know of any reason why a minor—a lad of about thirteen—shouldn't sign the Official Secrets Act declaration? You don't—there isn't any? Good. Thank you, my dear chap."

He rang off and turned back to Peregrene and Jonathan. "I don't think there can be any real objection," he said. "But first, sign this document please—both of you. It binds you to secrecy. There are serious penalties for any breach. Drastic penalties." The beam broadened. "Will you kindly both sit down?" They sat, and so did Sir Hartley, carefully crossing his legs and clasping his right knee with both hands. After a period of hesitation, Perry signed and then so did Jonathan.

The First Secretary continued to be disarmingly polite. "Thank you so much," he murmured. "Oh, and by the way, I will deny that this conversation ever took place if I have to." The beam had widened now to vast proportions.

"I think we've got the message," said Peregrene acidly.

"Excellent. I will keep what I have to say as brief as I can. For reasons we need not go into at present, I require your help to get an important man away from the borderlands of Kumaree and Nigella. His name is Ephraim Demir and he is in hiding. Or so we believe. It will be a fairly simple matter of flying in, unobserved of course, and flying out again with your passenger."

"What's he done, robbed a bank—or worse? Just who is this character, and who is he hiding from, and why?"

"Demir has been very helpful to my ministry. Extremely helpful. The gentleman we are talking about has, ah, supplied us with information of great international importance."

"I'm a simple man, Peers"—there was the rasp of irritation in Perry's voice now—"just a pilot-cum-businessman. Let's keep the talk very straight. If some guy has been doing the dirty to help you, then *you* get him out. You've got the whole of the air force behind you. For Pete's sake what has it got to do with me?"

"For a start, remember that we have flown together several times including that rather special occasion when we went under the bridge at Kringo. So I know your skill at first hand. Second, you will agree with me, I think, that Nigella is not the easiest of places to land an aircraft in the dark. But you are very familiar with the difficulties, aren't you, Mr Langhorne? I know you made many, many landings there not so long ago when you were on charter to Whole World Film Studios; not a bad one among them, I believe. Am I, ah, correct in supposing that there cannot be another pilot anywhere with your knowledge of the area?"

Perry shrugged. "I had help then, like lights and co-operation on the ground. But I'll tell you what I'll do: I'll pass on my information to one of your air force aces and he can go in to make the pick up at Table Mountain. How's that? And there'll be no charge for the service."

Sir Hartley, the beam reduced now to a smile of standard size, shook his head in disagreement. "That's not very practicable, is it? In any case, if you will ponder the consequences of failure for a moment you will surely see why we cannot use an air force plane or pilot. How embarrassing if the man were caught—embarrassing for this office and for the government. Why, we would be *implicated*!"

"Good grief!" said Perry. "And what about my embarrassment if *I'm* caught?" His usual rather leisurely drawl had quickened with indignation. "Exactly what happens to me?"

"The point is, you will not get caught. I have already assured the Minister and my colleagues here that you *can* do the job, that you *will* do it and that you will do it *successfully*. Success is essential; quite, quite essential. I have confidence in you and so, as a result, have all the other persons concerned. Now, if you don't co-operate . . ." the beam was lighting up again ". . . there are ways the government could fail to co-operate with you—in connection with, ah, for instance, ah, your licenced airfield."

A slow flush of anger had come to Perry's cheeks and he inclined forward, dangerously, towards the First Secretary. "Are you leaning on me?" he asked.

"Ah, on the other hand if you do co-operate, as I am wholly sure you are going to, there will be rich rewards." Peers was still batting with all the coolness of an ice pack, Perry's display of anger seeming to pass him by completely. "There will be the honour of having helped the country out of a particularly nasty predicament and there will, of course, be a fee; a handsome fee: ten thousand pounds, ah, for success. All expenses will be paid and all the facilities you need provided. Let me know in the morning—just in principle you understand—what your decision is. Then we can start on the details. Here are some spare Secrets Acts forms. If you use them make sure they are properly witnessed. By the way, speak as freely as you like in front of the chauffeur—he is a trusted man. Good day, gentlemen, good day."

But Perry, his feelings badly ruffled, was disinclined to talk much on the drive home. After a word or two to Charlie he lapsed into silence and the others followed suit, gazing at the passing countryside and thinking their own unspoken thoughts. At least the weather was improving. There were patches of blue sky now with big, white, fluffy cumulus clouds scudding along beneath. Shortly before four o'clock the car arrived at the field and stopped. They stepped out, muttered a word of thanks to the chauffeur and clambered up the steps to the tower where Roz was sitting, as usual, on radio watch. "Hi, there!" she said. "What's the matter with you lot?"

Perry grunted. "For one thing, we're hungry," he said. "They don't think of feeding you in Whitehall."

"Bad luck. Well, there's some bread and cheese in the cupboard there. Have that for the moment and I'll do a proper meal for all of us this evening. Oh, your friend Sir Hartley telephoned a few minutes ago. He wants you to call him back. Says it's very urgent. What's going on, Perry?"

"Be clear about one thing," replied Perry, settling himself into the one comfortable chair in the office: "Peers is no friend of mine. He's leaning on me—and I mean hard! There's some guy who's been spying for him in Kumaree, and I'm supposed to go out there to pick him up. I could . . ."

"*Perry!*" Jon was looking serious. "We've signed the secrets thing. We shouldn't be talking."

"Yeah, you're right Jonno. Roz and Charlie, sign here." He banged two blank forms on the table. "That means you go to jail if you gas to anyone who hasn't signed. It's a great system. Roz, send the forms to Peers will you—and don't forget to charge him for the stamp." When the signing had been done, Peregrene grumbled on.

"So, as I was saying, I'm supposed to pick this guy out of his rabbit hole. And I could get my nose bloodied in the action—as Peers is very well aware."

"In that case," said Roz breezily, "just don't do it."

"It isn't that simple." Perry folded his arms across his chest and rocked forward thoughtfully. "I know Peers. He puts leverage on people, real leverage. Then there happens to be a jackpot of a fee for the job—and you know the state of our accounts at present. We need the roubles. I'm darned if I know what we should do. Charlie, what do you think?"

Charlie was making the sandwiches, watched by Jon who had been noting how deftly the large hands sliced the bread. They were clumsy looking hands, but Charlie used them with all the delicacy and precision of an eye surgeon. "You haven't told me what the fee is yet," he said.

"Ten thousand and all expenses."

"Ten? Sainted Aunts, that's some charter! We'd better do it."

"Maybe. I wonder. Anyway, put the call through, will you Roz? I mean the call to my friend and admirer Sir Partly Here." Perry grinned. "Did you get that Jon? Sir Partly Here."

"Yes," said Roz. "He got that joke. Ha, ahem, ha."

Perry grinned more broadly than ever. He was looking more relaxed and like himself again.

Sir Hartley's voice sounded thinner and reedier than ever on the telephone, but still very bland. "I must be careful what I say, ah, in case the wrong ears overhear this conversation. But I thought you should know that shortly after you left I had a visit from, ah, a certain ambassador. Our friend, the one we discussed—no names no pack drill as they say—our friend *is* in hiding and there's one new twist. His son is being held. Just a lad, too. Only fifteen. Very sad. So there's another reason why you should do your stuff, if you follow me. A mission of mercy and all that. Now, you've had an hour or two to think and I take it that you *are* on for the exercise? We *can* rely on you?"

Perry's reply came over sounding pretty sour. "The way I take it is that I don't have a choice. So let's get on with the war."

"Splendid. Right, well, a man from the Ministry of Defence, a senior chap, is on his way to see you this evening. His name is Wilmot. He looks after CENTO matters here. You know about CENTO?"

"No."

"It's the Central Treaty Organisation. An important body. International. Wilmot will give you all the background you need. And he'll have a runner with him carrying a contract. Sign it please, and he'll return it to me. I'm afraid you can't have a copy—you'll just have to trust us. The car will arrive at, ah, say nine tonight."

"I should be here."

"You *will* be there, Langhorne! You must be there. A very, ah, good afternoon to you." The phone cut off and Perry replaced the receiver slowly, then turned to face the others. "I've known a few guys in my time," he said, "but never one like that. Listen, could he have a brain-lobe loose and still hold down that Whitehall job he's got?" But it wasn't a serious question. Nobody doubted that the Private Secretary to the Secretary of State had all his screws in place.

Roz-style cooking fell a little short of the standards of Cordon Bleu but she did a good job that night of steak, creamed potatoes and peas. They all ate well and talked in bursts about Sir Hartley's project. Lack of facts gave the situation a misty aura of unreality.

At just after nine-fifteen the ministry car arrived. Wilmot and the runner were taken into the dining room by Charlie. Jonathan eyed the visitors with interest. He'd expected the runner to be tough, young, possibly armed—and he wasn't any of these things; just a middle-aged, undersized man wearing a drab brown suit and carrying a brief-case chained to his wrist. At least the case looked its part—black and heavy, and decorated in gilt with the royal initials and a crown.

But Wilmot, of the MoD, had a presence to him, the sort of bearing that makes people take notice. He was tall and solid and seemed to carry an indefinable authority, like a top rank detective. He gave a quick little nod towards Perry. "Mr Langhorne?" he said, and Jonathan placed the voice at once: Australian—like his cousins from Melbourne.

Perry stood up slowly. "Yes, I'm Langhorne."

"Wilmot, Ministry of Defence." The man held forward a card of identity.

"Sit down," said Perry. "Let's talk. Somebody make some coffee."

Wilmot shook his head. "I'm sorry. The matter I have to speak about is confidential."

"Don't worry. They know about it. By the way, that's Roz, Charles and Jonathan. They've all signed the secrecy form. Here." He picked up the forms and handed them to Wilmot who seemed a little surprised and studied them carefully.

"Right," he said. "Thanks. I'll have these filed. This is the position then. Ephraim Demir, former Minister of the Interior of Kumaree, has done a bunk—defected. The President of Kumaree, General Cukurova—who's a very tough cookie indeed—believes he is either in Britain or on his way here.

Cukurova is demanding Demir's return."

Perry's keen eyes were watching Wilmot's face intently. "What's behind the defection?" he asked.

"Cukurova believes Demir has been passing information to various western powers."

"And has he?"

A suggestion of a smile came to Wilmot's lips. "I'm not at liberty to say," he replied. "Anyway, the British Government wishes to give Demir assistance. He is believed to be hiding out in a cave across the border in Nigella. You, Mr Langhorne, are asked to fly in to the area under cover of darkness to lift Demir away. You will be operating from RAF Akrotiri, in Cyprus. The mission, which is an extremely important one, has been code-named 'Operation Midnight' and will normally be referred to as 'Oscar Mike'. The target date for the picking-up is the night of 2nd August —three days' time."

Charlie looked surprised. "Good God!" he said. "That's quick."

"It is. It has to be."

Roz brought the coffee round and a pause in the talking set in. Then Perry put a question. "Am I right in assuming we take our own aircraft?"

"We believe you are operating an Aztec twin. It would be ideal. All fuelling arrangements and other facilities will be laid on."

"Okay. We'll take Yankee Foxtrot. Tell me, what happens if we make a little mistake somewhere and get caught?"

"I'm afraid you'll be disowned."

"How kind. And then?"

"It's hard to say. Cukurova is a dictator and unpredictable. He's ruthless, as you already know."

"This guy Demir. He *is* worth saving, is he? I mean apart from a few governments having red faces, Demir *is* worth the trouble of getting out?"

"Yes. Sure. Cukurova's a monster, and Demir wants to see the Kumareans free of him. Besides, Cukurova's climbing into bed with the communist powers while Demir's been pulling the other way —towards the western democracies. Towards us. NATO owes Demir a lot. We all do."

"What about Demir's son?"

Wilmot paused. "You know about Mahmut?"

"Sure. If that's his name."

"What do you know?"

"Just that the kid's being held in Kumaree."

Wilmot smiled and nodded briefly. "What you say does appear to be the case. It's a complication."

"So what have we got to do—bust him out of jail?"

"You'll be briefed on that—and other late developments—at Akrotiri. I wouldn't worry about Mahmut yet."

"Have you got the contract?"

The runner opened his big bag, took a folded paper out and handed it across. Charlie looked over Perry's shoulder and they read the document together. On acceptance, it said, an immediate, non-returnable payment of £2,000. On successful completion of the mission, the balance of £8,000 to follow within seven days. All operating expenses to be met.

"Jeeze, Perry!" said Charlie. "And just when I need some new pants."

Wilmot was holding out a pen. "Sign it please. Write 'I accept the Operation Midnight offer' across the foot, and sign. Yes, that's it—there."

"Yeah," murmured Perry. "Yeah. I understand. I'm going to be somebody's breakfast soon." Taking out his pen he wrote the acceptance slowly and neatly on the foot of the form, and signed.

"Good. I'm afraid you can't have a copy for . . ."

"I know. I've just got to trust you."

Wilmot smiled again, quite a warm smile in all the circumstances, and handed the contract to the runner. "When can you leave?" he asked Perry.

"In the morning. Maybe. We'll flight test the aircraft in the morning and if it's all okay we'll take off at noon."

"That's fine. I'd, er, like to wish you good luck." He held out his hand and Perry shook it. "Thanks buster," he said. And within a few minutes the visitors left.

As soon as the ministry car drove off into the darkness, Jonathan began his campaign. "I'm coming too," he said. "*Definitely.*" Then, a little less sure of himself—"Please."

Charlie grinned and tweaked the boy's nose playfully. "Growing lads shouldn't be out mixing it with spies and dictators," he said. "They should be going to bed early and doing their homework."

"Please!"

Perry was already beginning to look out charts and

gear for the flight. "You can come as far as Cyprus, Jonny," he said. "But clear it with your mother first. Right?"

"You bet." And about twelve seconds later Mrs Kane rose to answer the 'phone, and in about another twelve had been talked into saying Yes.

There was a sniff of action in the night air. Exhilarating stuff.

Chapter Two

CALL THE TOWER AND GO

Jon clambered up to his attic bedroom at twenty-two minutes to twelve. He put on his pyjamas, yawned twice while doing so, switched off the light, then went to the little window that faced south across the field. Yankee Foxtrot, the old Aztec B, was standing there looking mysterious and exciting in the dark. Sometimes it seemed to Jon that an aeroplane had a personality of its own—a sort of soul. You could imagine it almost knowing things as it grew older and chalked up more and more adventures in the air. Yankee Foxtrot had seen some action in her time—and she was going to see a lot more right now. She looked very much at peace, standing there in the gentle night time breeze, utterly silent, her two big fans just discernable with the blades neatly parked east/west, parallel to the distant skyline. "Have a good night's rest, Yankee Foxtrot," he mused to himself. "You've got a busy day coming tomorrow."

But that went for him, too, he realised as he climbed into bed. He planned to play a full part in the flight out—Perry and Charlie would be tired and glad of his help. So he must sleep to be fresh and alert in the morning. He closed his eyes and commanded sleep to come, which it did not do. "Now come on," he told himself two or three minutes later, "relax—and sleep!" He lay for a while on his left side, then on his right, then on his back, then again on the left side. The truth was he was pretty jangled up thinking of the day ahead. A full fourteen hours of continuous day and night flying, Perry had reckoned, plus three refuelling stops of about an hour each. Seventeen hours! It was an awesome thought. With luck he'd spend a few of those hours in the right hand seat. Yankee Foxtrot's auto pilot never worked properly so the aircraft would have to be hand flown every mile of the way. There was work enough for three pilots there. "For Heaven's sake," he thought, "am I never going to sleep?" He flipped over to his right side again. Perry would still be downstairs, working on the charts—so he would be tired tomorrow too. Some crew they were going to be; dead beat before they even took off. He settled down to the old boring business of counting imaginary sheep jumping over a hedge. Then Charlie was shaking him, shaking him and shaking him some more. "Come on, Jonno, come on. Wake up! Holy smoke, what a sleeper you are. Come on mate—wake up!"

Jon opened his eyes with an effort to see Charlie's big shape grinning down at him. "Come on Captain, we've got to get airborne. Let's go."

Charlie looked pretty good—fresh and ready for action. Consciousness, the recollection that this was the big day, flooded back into Jonathan's mind. "Thanks, Charlie," he muttered. "Thanks. I was tired." He rolled out of bed and stretched. "What's the time?"

"Nine o'clock. And at nine-thirty we flight test Yankee Foxtrot—that's you and me. Keep moving, mate."

"I'll be down in five minutes."

Charlie ambled away whistling a tuneless version of Tin Roof Blues. He seemed happy about the long hop to Cyprus; a seventeen hour trip made a change, of course, and it also made some money.

Jon raced downstairs comfortably inside the five minute forecast by cutting out non-essentials like washing, and combing hair. In the kitchen he met Perry, who was looking in good form after all. "Morning, Jon," he said cheerfully. "Boil yourself an egg. Better make it two eggs, maybe three—I don't know when you'll be eating again."

"Okay, thanks. I'll have two. Have you got the flight plan ready?"

"I surely have. We stop at Lyon, Naples, Athens then Akrotiri—the RAF field. Take off at noon GMT, land somewhere about six in the morning, Cyprus time. Just right for breakfast. Sounds easy—doesn't it?"

"It sounds great."

"Now listen, here's the programme I suggest for you. First, breakfast. Then help Charlie flight test Yankee Foxtrot. Then get yourself ready for the trip. What are you taking?"

"I don't know. I haven't thought about it."

"Well, remember, it's going to be hot—and I mean *very* hot. Don't bring much, because we want to travel as light as possible, but put in some swimming shorts. You're in for a pleasant day or two on the beach."

Jon's eager expression faded a little at the mention of the beach. He didn't care to be reminded that while Perry and Charlie were involved in the action, he was to be relegated to swimming from Limmasol beach. "I haven't got my swimming stuff here," he said flatly.

"You'll have an hour after the flight test to ride home for it. So do that. If anyone's looking for me I'll be in the tower." He strolled out of the kitchen leaving Jon to make himself a hurried breakfast.

Outside, one of those beautiful soft summer days was developing; blue and white sky, bright sunshine, a refreshing breeze and the sweet smell of the grass. As Jon walked towards the Aztec, carrying his two small inflatable cushions—one to sit on, the other to stuff behind him—he saw Charlie at the aircraft closing and locking the starboard engine inspection cowl. "Good," said Charlie, "you've been quick. Let's DI the aircraft." So the pre-flight Daily Inspection that a good pilot always makes, the slow walk round checking everything that matters, began. Charlie, Chief Instructor at the struggling 20-member flying club based at Lonehead Field, was always thorough about his routines. "Don't wait until you're in the air to find you've got a jammed control or water in the fuel," he used to say. "It can affect your health."

They went round together. "Start at the entry door," said Charlie, "and tell me what you're doing."

Jon threw his cushions inside, then moved towards the rear of the aircraft, standing on his toes one minute, stooping forward the next, gazing critically at the fuselage top, side and bottom surfaces. "I'm making sure there's no damage," he explained, "and nothing hanging off. It all looks okay to me. Now I'm checking the tail plane, again for damage, and for full and free movement."

"Call it a 'stabilator'," corrected Charlie. "D'you know the difference?"

Jon hesitated, then came up with the answer. "Yep. An ordinary tail plane is fixed with moving elevators on the rear edge. With a stabilator, the whole unit moves."

"Absolutely right. Go on, Chief."

Jon grasped the stabilator and waggled it up and down. "It seems fine," he said, then moved his attention to the fin. "There's nothing wrong here, either," he said. "The rudder doesn't move much but that's only because it's linked to the steering nosewheel." Charlie nodded.

They went on round the tail assembly and back up along the other side of the fuselage, their eyes ranging over the skin and fixings searching for defects. Yankee Foxtrot seemed to be in good shape, as Jon had fully expected.

They arrived at the wing root, port side. The flap was down and Jon gave it a vigorous shake. "Nothing wrong there," he said.

"Okay, but have a good look at the hydraulic levers that move it. Are you sure they're connected?"

Jonathan crouched to study the assembly. "Yes, they're connected," he replied. "It all looks good."

"Right, let's move on."

Next they turned to the aeleron. "No damage here," said Jon lifting it up, then pushing it down, "and full and free movement again." Round the wing tip they went, checking top and bottom surfaces, then along past the leading edge of the wing, pausing at the tube-like pitot head slung under the wing and jutting into the slipstream. "Pitot's okay. The cover's off and there's no blockage," remarked Jon.

"Good news. By the way, exactly what does the pitot head do?"

Jon looked irritably up at Charlie. "Remember I'm not a beginner, Charlie," he said icily. "It senses the air pressure and gives a speed reading in the cockpit."

Charlie laughed and gave him a gentle shake on the shoulder. "Yeah, I'm sorry Captain. I forgot you were the ace. Come on, let's hurry up with the rest, check the engines for oil and loose connections, the landing gear, the starboard wing—and then we'll see if we can fly the thing."

They finished the DI where they had started it, by the single entry door. "You start up, Jonno," said Charlie unexpectedly. "I'll get the fuel bowser going. Can you taxi over to me?"

"You bet."

"Okay. Be quick and be *careful.*" Charlie walked off and Jon climbed happily in through the Aztec's only door on the right, slid across the co-pilot's seat and settled himself on his cushions in the captain's place on the left. Now for the joy of bringing those silent Lycomings to throbbing life. The port engine first.

To begin with he pressed the toe brakes firmly on and locked them by pulling a tee-shaped toggle on the left of the panel, then reached down to the fuel cocks on the floor between the two front seats and selected "on". Next he put his finger on the left of two small fuel pump switches above his left knee and flicked it up; nothing happened. Why not? Where was the rapid clicking sound of the pump lifting fuel to the carburettor? Jonathan glanced round the cockpit in confusion for a moment and then yes, yes, of course, the master switch was still off. He found it forward and low, beneath the instrument panel, and switched on. The click-click-clicking began, the panel needles flicked up to give their readings and the gyros started to hum. Lines of tension on the boy's face relaxed into a smile. Yankee Foxtrot was coming to life.

He turned his attention to the battery of black, green and red knobs on the throttle consul. They were arranged in three pairs—black throttles to the left, green pitch levers in the centre, and red mixture controls to the right. He moved the left pitch control forward into fully fine and the left mixture knob also forward to rich. Now, taking the left throttle in his hand, he pumped it briskly forwards and backwards six times to prime the cylinders with fuel. He brought the throttle back to about a quarter open. "Just don't let me down," he whispered. "Start."

The start switch serving both engines was located quite high up on the instrument panel. It was a simple projecting rod of metal an inch or so long. He took the rod-like switch between his finger and thumb, pulled it out, and moved it left. At once the left propeller began to rotate but slowly and jerkily; you would have thought with reluctance. "Come on, Yankee Foxtrot," said Jon coaxingly, "get a move on." Then, suddenly, the engine fired and the propeller was revving rapidly, the big Lycoming giving out with its powerful roar, and the airframe quivering with forward urge against the brakes. Jon grinned contentedly and set the throttle for 1,500 rpm. Forty seconds later the starboard engine was running too. To Jon's ears it was music they made together, the noisy, thrilling harmonics of mechanical power from well tuned aero engines. He switched the booster fuel pumps off and the generators on. The big fans were throwing the airstream backwards at a rate that flattened the grass for yards behind them. Jon let them blast away for a minute or so while the Lycomings warmed up. Then he throttled back to a thousand, released the brakes and Yankee Foxtrot began to roll.

Over to the right, beyond the house, Charlie was standing by the 100 octane fuel bowser, the filler nozzle in his hand. Slowly, carefully, Jonathan rolled towards him, stopped at an angle of about forty five degrees to the bowser and clamped on the brakes. Charlie moved a thumb across his throat, the universally understood sign for "cut". Jon cut, by pulling the mixture controls back to fully lean. In three or four seconds the big Lycomings stopped. Next, the switches all went off and there was silence but for the declining whine of the gyros slowing down. He hopped out to help Charlie. The bowser's pumping engine was the only sound now—and it seemed pretty feeble by comparison.

There were four wing tanks to fill and it took a few minutes to do. With a hundred and twenty gallons on board, a full load, they shut the bowser off and climbed in, Charlie in the left hand seat, Jon acting co-pilot on the right.

"You do the work—I'll just watch," said Charlie. "D'you remember the checks mnemonic?" The touch of authority was coming back to Charlie again, the flying instructor manner that meant there was only one way to do anything—the right way. Jon knew to be careful now, and to concentrate. He nodded.

"T T M P F F G G H H," he said.

"Meaning?"

"Trim, throttle, Mixture, Pitch, Fuel, Flap, Gyros, Gauges, Hatches and Harness."

"All right, Captain. Start the engines. Left then right."

They started easily and a happy smile that he was quite unaware of spread across Jonathan's face. "They sound great," he said. "Marvellous."

"No need to be a poet about it," said Charlie cuttingly. "Now, look, taxi clear of the bowser and we'll do the run up and checks. Keep an eye on that wing tip—you're a bit close for my liking. Let's have power on the left engine and a dab on the right hand toe brake. Come on." Jon revved up on the left engine and dabbed away at the right rudder pedal toe brake. Yankee Foxtrot swung right, safely clear of obstructions, and Jon levelled the throttles so that the aircraft taxied steady and straight towards the take off point for grass runway two-two. On the way, after clearing the house and hangar, they stopped to run up the engines and go through the pre-flight checks. Trim levers set for take off, throttle friction nut firm, mixture fully rich and no carburettor heat, pitch fully fine, fuel selected and booster pumps on, flap in take off position, gyros and gauges functioning correctly, hatches and harness secure.

"Okay," said Charlie. "Call the tower and let's go." Jonathan pulled the boom mike into position, pressed the transmit button on the control column and made his call. "Lonehead. Yankee Foxtrot. Ready to line up."

Roz's cool voice came back at once. "Yankee Foxtrot line up. Take off at your discretion."

Jon hesitated. "Acknowledge," said Charlie gruffly. "Then roll out and line up." Again Jon pressed the button. "Yankee Foxtrot," he said, and with his left hand put on the power. He turned the aircraft into wind and stopped, the throttles back at fast tick-over speed. There was another pause.

"Is everything okay?" asked Charlie.

"I think so."

"Go ahead then. Take off."

Jon turned to look at him anxiously. "Me?" he said.

"Sure."

"Well, will you put your hands and feet on too?"

"You bet I will, if I have to. Go ahead."

Very suddenly Jon's heart began to pound and knock like a high speed hammer. Charlie's arms were folded and his feet tucked back almost under the seat which made the message plain. He was to do it alone. Well, he mustn't be chicken about it. He put his left hand on the throttles and began to move them smoothly, rapidly forward. The Lycomings responded at once with a thunderous roar and Jon felt a shove in the small of his back. Yankee Foxtrot was away like a bolting horse across the field, thumping a bit over the rougher patches of ground. You could feel the acceleration pushing you into the seat.

Early in the take off run Charlie shouted some advice. "Get the weight off that nose wheel! Quick, let's have back pressure on the stick." Keeping his left hand on the throttles Jon eased the column back with his right, and the ride smoothed out as the quivering nosewheel all but floated on the grass. His heart was still banging twenty-five to the dozen and he wished Charlie's help would go further than words. He glanced far left, awkwardly so, towards the air speed indicator above Charlie's left knee and saw the needle swinging round past the sixty mark. The boundary hedge was coming towards them at the gallop now and he eased further back on the stick, willing Yankee Foxtrot into the air. She tried twice, giving little bounds with all wheels off, then she was back in contact with the grass again, hell-bent on clipping the hedge, until suddenly, smoothly, they were off and away, airborne. The hedge whipped past underneath and they were climbing at ninety. "That's good," yelled Charlie. "Get the gear in quickly."

Jon took his hand off the throttles and groped down on the lower right side of the throttle console for the undercarriage lever, a wheel shaped knob. He found it, had a quick glance down to confirm that he had what he thought he had in his hand, then pulled upwards. The knob wouldn't come. Ah, yes, he remembered the little safety gate that had to be pulled aside. "Use the brakes," chided Charlie. "The wheels are still spinning." Charlie was beginning to look restive at the fumbling, then the lever came up and the three green lights below the throttles went out, giving way to one yellow. The wheels were safely up and tucked away.

"Watch your speed—hold her at a hundred and five knots," said Charlie. "Come on, stick back a bit. And get your flap in."

Jon felt the cool sweat on his face again. There was a lot to do on take off. He knew now, knew very well, what professional pilots meant by their phrase, "cleaning up the cockpit". He put his hand down again, this time to the other side of the throttle console feeling for the flaps lever—this one shaped like a little bit of wing section. He found it, glanced quickly to be sure, and selected "up".

"Keep watching your speed. You're fast now. Start a left turn and call the tower that you're leaving the circuit."

Jon began a turn, wiped the sweat from his eyes with the back of his right hand, then pressed the transmit button. "Yankee Foxtrot leaving the circuit."

"Yankee Foxtrot," Roz came back with her usual clipped efficiency. Her "cucumber voice" Perry often called it. Jon liked to hear her on the air, especially when they were pushing back through soupy weather.

"The turn's too steep—check it." Charlie was still sounding gruff. "Don't let it build up on you. That's better. Let's straighten up anyway. Steer zero-one-zero and level out at three thousand." Jon was too slow to correct the altitude of the aircraft so that they gained some excess height and too slow to take off bank so that they swung through to three-six-zero before ending the turn. He began to make corrections looking flustered and unhappy, grinding his teeth behind lips set in a thin straight line, and still sweating.

Then Charlie laughed and clapped him on the knee with his big heavy hand. "You're doing all right, Captain," he said. "Just a little rusty. Let's enjoy it." The tension broke immediately and Jon settled down to his course and height.

"Bring the throttles back about a quarter—we

want a manifold pressure of twenty-three inches." Jon eased them back.

"Good. Now the pitch levers back to about twenty-three hundred revs." The engines throbbed as they ran out of phase at differing rpm until both pitch levers were back, and the engines balanced, first the port control, then starboard. "All right Chief," said Charlie. "We're all sorted out." They were cruising at 180 and the "cleaning up" was done.

They put Yankee Foxtrot through a few semi-steep turns—rates two to three—checked the engine temperatures and pressures and found everything good. Charlie turned to Jonathan. "I think she's ready for Cyprus, don't you?"

"Yes. She seems great."

"But we'll just feather the engines in turn, before we go back. Okay?"

That was a new drill for Jon and he was keen to see it. He nodded agreement.

"I expect you know that by 'feather' we mean turning the props edgeways into the slipstream to stop them windmilling. But d'you know why we do it?" Charlie was being the serious minded flying instructor again.

"Yes. To reduce the drag. There's more drag when a propeller's windmilling than when it's feathered."

"Right. Getting rid of the drag is important when you're flogging along on one engine. And if there's something mechanical wrong with it you might damage it more by letting it spin. So let's feather. I'll do your side first. Are your feet firmly on the rudder?"

"Yes."

"Be ready for lots of swing—see if you can hold her straight when the engine goes out. Now, I'm feathering the starboard engine, so which way will she turn?"

"To the right."

"Right. And you'll need a real bootful of left rudder to hold her. Now, all we do is to pull back the three engine controls from left to right. First the throttle—you all set?" Jon nodded, feeling tense again, and Charlie pulled the starboard throttle lever fully back. Immediately Yankee Foxtrot began a sharp, skidding turn right and Charlie moved the port throttle forward to maximum cruise power. The skidding grew rapidly worse. Jon pushed forward with his left foot to counteract the turn and found it took a lot of muscle, just about all he had. He got his knee locked straight with his leg fully extended and was just about holding her.

"Now I'm working systematically from left to right," went on Charlie. "We've got the starboard throttle closed. Next in line is the pitch lever—this green knob. I'm going to pull it fully back to the feather. By the way—see the light flashing in the undercarriage selector knob? That's a warning that you've lost power." He grinned: "I reckon the rudder's already given you that information though."

"It takes a heck of a lot of holding." Jon was grinding his teeth again with the effort. "Can I use the rudder trim?"

"In a minute. We don't usually—we just do it the hard way and head for the nearest airfield to get down. All right, back with the pitch lever to 'feather'. Now, look at the prop." It had stopped. There was something quite odd about the propeller's appearance, motionless in flight. Jon, beginning to sweat again with the sheer physical effort of holding course, nodded an acknowledgement.

"So now for the last of the engine controls—the mixture." Charlie reached for the red knob and pulled it back like the others. "There we are—fully lean. The starboard engine is feathered."

Jon was beginning to lose his battle with the rudder. "You'll have to develop a bit more leg power, Captain," said Charlie blandly. "Try some knees-bend exercises."

"No thanks. But I can't hold her much longer. I'll have to use the trim." Jon was increasingly uncomfortable. Then Charlie's own large boot went on to the pedal and the strain came off. "I'll trim for you," he said amiably. "Look at the speed."—He tapped the ASI—"We're holding about a hundred and ten knots. That's not bad on one is it? Now, let's unfeather the engine. You do it. Just work through the controls in reverse order—red, green, black —then use the starter."

Jon pushed the red mixture control to rich, the pitch to fine, the throttle partly open and the start switch to the right. "Good," said Charlie. "Now watch." The propeller was windmilling round, picking up speed. But it was some time, a long-feeling six or seven seconds, before the big Lycoming began to work. Then it fired and after a period of rough running was pulling properly.

"Now throttle back," said Charlie as soon as it did so. "Look at your temperature gauges—how do they read?"

Jon studied the array of flickering needles in front of him. The temperature gauges would be to the right, among the engines' instruments on the co-pilot's side, flight instruments being positioned left facing Charlie. So. But where? He saw everything else, the guages he didn't need, like vacuum suction for the gyros, flap setting indicator, fuel and oil pressures and then, ah yes, low down he found the oil temperatures. He glanced over to Charlie. "Oil temperature is low for the starboard engine. Just about off the clock."

"That's it. Full marks, Captain Jon. A feathered engine goes cold very fast in the slipstream. So when you bring it in again, nurse it for a couple of minutes until it's warm."

They feathered the port engine next and Charlie explained that when that engine went out, so did the hydraulics. "So to lower the flaps and gear you have to do a little work," he said. "See this knob? Well, pull it."

Jon reached for the large red knob, another one that stuck out of the throttles consul, pointing rearwards, and was surprised to find that it pulled out a long way, about a foot. "Now you've got a pump handle in your hand," explained Charlie. "If your hydraulics are out, select flaps or gear down in the ordinary way, then get to work pumping with that. It'll make you sweat, mate, although I don't suppose you'll ever have to use it." He tucked it back in and unfeathered the port engine. "And there's one other trick," he said. "Under my seat here there's a little plate with a wing nut—have a look."

Jon undid his seat belt, leaned with difficulty across Charlie's right thigh and peered awkwardly under the seat.

"D'you see it?"

"Yes."

"Well, in a real emergency, you open the lid and pull a D ring you'll find inside. That fires a nitrogen bottle and everything goes down with a bang—gear, flaps, the lot. And I do mean with a bang. Well, let's find the field. Call for rejoining."

Jon pressed the transmit button. "Lonehead. Yankee Foxtrot rejoining from the north. Landing instructions please."

"Yankee Foxtrot, runway two-two, QFE niner-niner-niner. Call finals." It was Roz again and the cucumber voice was coming through loud and clear. Jon could imagine her walking over as she often did to put the coffee on to greet them. He pressed to transmit again. "Two-two," he said reading the message back. "Niner-niner-niner. Thank you."

Jon made the approach with a little help, whistling towards the boundary hedge at 85 knots. "It always looks a small field," he said, "especially for the Aztec."

"It darned well *is* a small field," agreed Charlie putting his hands and feet on. "So keep her low. You're too high. That's it, power off a bit and stick forward. And you want eighty on the clock as we cross the fence." A cow was grazing placidly in the undershoot area, a neighbouring field, and Jon wondered at its indifference to two and a bit tonnes of Aztec steaming towards it and evidently bent on parting the animal's hair.

They touched down very gently with the tail nice and low, and pounded across the field on the long landing roll. Jon was wild about flying, loved every God-given minute of it, yet there was always something pleasing, reassuring about the feel of the ground under the wheels after a flight. He settled back against his cushions and relaxed as Charlie dabbed at the brakes and the far hedge began to look very close. It was twelve minutes past ten. One hour and forty-eight minutes until take-off time for Akrotiri and the sun. They topped up the tanks and taxied back to park Yankee Foxtrot near the hangar.

Just inside the front door of the house Perry had gathered an assortment of bits and pieces wanted for the trip. There were three life jackets, a collection of maps and radio charts, his bulging flight brief case, an overnight bag and a tin box of sandwiches thoughtfully prepared by Roz. He wandered out of the dining room wearing a light-weight, casual zip-up jacket and sharply pressed blue cotton drill trousers; a neat, you might even say dapper figure of slightly less than average height, slimly built and fit looking, with brown sinewy hands and a lean tanned face that had a flick of humour about the eyes and mouth. "Hi," he said as the other two came in, "how's the aeroplane?"

"It seems all right, pretty good," said Charlie. "We're all fuelled up and ready to go. But what's the pretty gear for? Is the Queen coming or something?"

"Almost. Sir Hartley actually. He's coming to see us off, so don't forget to wash behind your ears. Jon, get ready for the road. I've looked you out some swimming shorts—mine. They're on your bed."

A shadowy frown showed briefly on Jon's face. "They'll be too big," he said.

"They're elastic. They'll do. And you'll want some pyjamas and a toothbrush. Come on, let's move. We'll get all the gear ready and down, then have a cup of coffee and run through the flight plan. Okay?"

At eleven-fifteen they gathered with Roz in the tower and Perry put the flight log, carefully filled up with his own small, precise writing, on the table. "First hop, then," he said in his drawly voice, "is to Lyon. Distance five hundred and thirty-two nautical miles, flight time three hours thirty-three minutes—we'll call that three hours forty at one-five-five knots cruise speed—and an altitude of nine thousand. We'll use about eighty-eight gallons on the leg and since we're carrying a hundred and twenty we've a good reserve. Is everyone happy with that?" Charlie and Jon both nodded.

"Good. Charlie, you fly in the right hand seat to Lyon, Jon you can take care of the maps in the back.

We're going out on Airway Amber One to Moulins, then Amber Two. We have a light easterly wind—it's about zero-nine-five at ten—and our expected time of arrival at Lyon is fifteen thirty-three. We'll be crossing nearish the Alps, so let's not hit one. I think we're ready to go—drink up." Then, as he finished speaking, a faint tapping came from the half open office door and a reedy voice was calling out: "Are you there, Mr Langhorne?" it said. "Shall I just come in? Good morning, good morning." At that moment Sir Hartley's beaming face appeared in the tower, as pink and healthy as ever. "Aha, coffee," he went on. "I'm in luck. Well, how are you all this excellent morning? Ready for the sun, eh?"

Perry nodded briefly. "Come in, Peers," he said. "I guess we're about ready to go. Take a seat. Roz, can you do another coffee?" The words themselves were friendly enough, as friendly as the occasion called for perhaps, but there was an edge to Perry's voice, an uncharacteristic coolness that everyone noticed at once. "Are you coming along for the ride, then?" he added. "Can they spare you from the paper chase at Whitehall?"

"Ah, I fear not. I'm needed. Busy all the time. But we have a man at Akrotiri who'll give you every assistance. No thank you, no sugar—fattening at my age you know, ha ha. Yes, now where was I, ah yes, the man's name is Fenwick Pinkerton. You can put your confidence in him without reservation. Absolutely without reservation. He's one of us—knows the ropes."

Pinkerton, thought Perry. Pinkerton! It would be a name like that. And "one of us". Us! Good God! He fought off a strong desire to be rude to the smooth, the smiling, the urbane, the polished, the indestructible, the arm-twisting Sir Hartley, who had come so graciously to see them off into a situation they didn't want to be in and might very well not come out of in one piece. "Right," he said quietly. "We'll be looking for Mr Pinkerton in seventeen hours at Akrotiri. You can send him a wire."

Sir Hartley escorted them across to the Aztec. They stowed their gear, said goodbye to Roz, who beseeched them to be careful and to hurry back, then climbed aboard. With fast practiced movements Peregrene and Charlie had the Lycomings throbbing powerfully, and Yankee Foxtrot began to roll. There was a brief pause near the threshold of runway two-two as the engines came up one by one to three-quarters power for a mag-drop check, then they turned into wind and in a quick crescendo of noise were away. When Perry did a take off it was a sight to see: A straight roll down the middle running, you would think, on invisible rails; smooth and rapid acceleration; then the nose up a little and then a little more and a clean lift off, the gear coming up maybe three seconds later; then at 300 feet the flaps sliding briskly away, and then there they were, climbing fast into the blue summer sky and turning onto one-six-two on the first course for Lyon. Roz felt lonely and a little sad as Yankee Foxtrot shrank into the distance. Sir Hartley was surprisingly pleasant as they walked back together—almost sympathetic in an unemotional sort of way. For one thing the smile had gone, and that made a difference.

Jon settled himself down in the seat behind Charlie and spread out the first map. He felt a curious inner tingling, a suspense. The sensation was acute and not pleasant. He didn't believe in premonitions—he well knew the future never showed its cards ahead of time. Yet he had the strongest feeling about dramatic things going to happen. And to him. He wouldn't be swimming on the beach, he was totally sure of that. And he felt something else centred down in the pit of the stomach, something he was honest enough to identify.

Fear.

Chapter Three

RUN—GET OUT

Ephraim Demir, a smallish, tidy-looking man with a neat black moustache and dark complexion, had first heard of his unmasking while sitting at his large, green-topped ministerial desk at ten-fifteen in the morning two days before the Aztec set course for Lyon and Akrotiri. He was half way through a confidential memo from Yasar Cukurova, "the General", on the subject of public order. In Cukurova's view there wasn't enough of it and, as he bluntly pointed out, it was Ephraim's responsibility, as Minister of the Interior, to sort the situation out. "A degree of toughness seems to be called for," the general wrote. "A well publicised hanging or two could do much to restore the sense of patriotism to our people. I look for a rapid improvement in public morale and behaviour. Act quickly."

To the just and gentle Ephraim, Cukurova's words made wretched reading. He cast his eyes back over the central sentence. A hanging or two! Maybe three, maybe ten. Other people's lives. Take them when you want, take them at the whim of policy and take them brutally. How much longer until the general's relentless claws could be clipped? Progress was so slow, so very much too slow. He cupped his chin in his hands and gazed across the spacious office to the opposite wall. Cukurova looked back at him in portrait form, dressed, as usual, in the sparkling white tunic of the Kumarean officers, three rows of medal ribbons on his chest. Ephraim studied the general's eyes and marvelled again at the coldness and arrogance he saw in them. The face was strong, a little fleshy now at forty, but reflecting well the confidence and, yes, it had to be admitted, the courage of the man behind it.

Then the telephone rang, intruding on his thoughts. Ephraim lifted the receiver. "Demir," he said.

"Ephraim, are you alone?" The words came over as a whisper, rushed and agitated.

"Who's that?" Ephraim felt a flash of apprehension as he put the question.

"For heaven's sake!" the voice replied. "Are you *alone*?"

"Yes."

"Then listen. Cukurova knows about the plot. He's on to you. Run. Get out now."

The colour drained from Ephraim's cheeks. "But how?" he asked in a voice suddenly and strangely changed. "How can Cukurova know about us?"

"You heard what I said. Get out *now*." The caller hung up abruptly.

Ephraim, trembling, shocked by the suddenness

and nature of the call, put the receiver back, rose and without a backward look left the office. He hurried along the corridor, down a flight of stairs and out past the sentry into the sunny street. Walking quickly and with lowered head he turned left into a pleasant residential road, and then left again through an open gate that led him into a fine secluded garden and towards a large, stone built house of impressive appearance. Climbing three steps, he rang the bell of the front door and waited. A servant soon appeared, recognised Ephraim, bowed slightly and ushered him into the house. "Please tell Pasha Kanik that I am here," said Ephraim. "Convey my regret for calling unannounced. It is an important matter that I have come about."

Moments later he was taken to a huge, comfortably furnished room to be warmly greeted by Kanik, a handsome though ageing man of fully six feet tall with sallow cheeks and a bushy, white moustache. "Why, my dear old friend, what brings you here so early in the day?" asked Kanik. "I have sent for coffee and retsina. Let us sit together over there." He pointed to a long, low couch. "You look unwell. Is something wrong?"

"I can only stay a moment," said Ephraim sitting down. "You'll understand why. Kanik, my friend, my trusted friend, the plot is known. Cukurova has found out. I have just been told of it."

"Who told you?" Kanik looked serious but unafraid.

"I'm not sure. The message came by 'phone. It

could have been Zeid. His voice was strangely thick—I would say the voice of a man possessed by fear. What is your advice, Kanik? Tomorrow I think I will be dangling from a rope."

Kanik nodded his calm, wise head in agreement. "That is always Cukurova's answer, but it must not happen. Get away at once. You will do the cause no good in death. How much do you think is known?"

"I truly cannot say. The call was very short."

"Zeid, you think it was?"

"It could have been."

"Zeid is a good man but too fearful. Life is hard on such people."

The servant returned with two cups of thick black coffee, glasses and a bottle of retsina wine, all on a silver tray which he placed on a knee-high table. Kanik waved the man away with a fluttering gesture of the hand. "Probably less is known than you think," he went on when the door had closed behind the servant. "History is full of people who brought disaster on themselves by believing in their downfall prematurely. I urge you to go, but the rest of us must stay here, just as we are, steadfast. Do you still have your visions, Ephraim? Do you still see our Kumaree of the future, free, prospering, happy, culturally fulfilled, taking its place—as you used to say—as a leader nation in the world?"

"I still have them, Kanik. More vividly, I think, than ever."

"Then live. Be our leader in exile. Get out of Kumaree with your neck intact. The western powers will help you once you cross the border. And you will come back some day to take your place as head of state. You will find us here, waiting."

"Whatever happens, Kanik, I shall never be able to repay you for all you have done in the years we have worked together."

Kanik smiled broadly, so broadly that the ends of his lips disappeared beneath his huge moustache. "I'm too old to worry about repayments, my friend," he said. "It's one of the compensations. Go now. I will see Zeid to calm him down."

"I have one last favour to ask: Mahmut, my boy. He is now fifteen and, as you know, at school in England . . ."

"That is good. He will be safe."

"No, Kanik. Fate is against me at present. Mahmut leaves today by air to spend his holidays with me at my house in Konyak. A great misfortune. I planned to meet him this afternoon. Now, somehow, I must tell Ismet, my servant, to be at Lusquat Airport at three this afternoon. Flight three-two-three, Kumarean Airways. Ismet can bring the boy to me."

"What about your wife? Where is she? What does she know?"

"You remember Dorothy, Kanik! She is in New York or London—as usual. Anywhere but here. She has never liked it here. Always the weather is wrong—too hot, too cold, too windy; something! Too hard on her health whatever it does. Poor Dorothy, she is always worried about her health. You remember? Anyway, she knows nothing of our struggle.

Nothing."

"You will be at the cave? The one fifteen miles across the border in Nigella?"

"Yes, the one near Table Mountain. I believe it is still secure, and even contains survival rations. I will stay there as long as necessary."

"It must be sixty miles or more from here."

"I walk well, Kanik. And perhaps I will be given lifts."

"This Ismet—he knows the cave, and is to be trusted?"

"Yes, he knows it. And Ismet is loyal. I trust him fully. But how to reach him as things are?"

"You have the telephone at Konyak?"

"Yes, but a call may well be overheard. Our telephone system has always been like a market place."

"Then I will call. I will say that I hear you are on your way to, to, yes to Bucharest on government business. I will ask him to call here to collect some papers for your personal and immediate attention on your return. No one will interfere with that. And when he comes I will send him on to Lusquat Airport. Now, my friend, you must go. Here, wear these."

From a heavily ornamented cupboard Kanik took out a dark wig of short hair, a stick-on moustache also dark but otherwise a scaled down version of his own exuberant display, a raincoat of undistinguished appearance and a peaked cloth cap. "And go out this way, by the garden. You will not be seen."

Kanik began to smile again at the sight of the Minister of the Interior dressed up in the rough clothes of a workman, and then the smile froze and quickly disappeared. The two men embraced warmly and a moment later Ephraim stepped out through the side door and was gone.

If Ismet was surprised to be telephoned by the famous Pasha Kanik, one of Kumaree's richest and most respected citizens, he showed no sign of it. "I will come at once," he said.

"It must be twelve miles, Ismet. Is there a car you can use?"

"No, Pasha, cars are not for me."

"How will you come? How long will it take?"

"We have a strong horse and a four-wheeled cart. It will carry me to you within an hour, Pasha."

"You are a good servant, Ismet. I would like these papers to be given to Pasha Demir the moment he returns from Bucharest. They tell me at the ministry that that should be soon, perhaps tomorrow." He hung up and stood for a while at the window enjoying the peace of the fruitful garden and pondering the future.

When Ismet was brought into the house he stood awkwardly before Kanik, his cloth cap crumpled tightly in his hand, bowing and embarrassed. He had not expected to be received in person by a man as great as this and in the splendour of the sitting room. "I would have dressed more finely, Pasha . . . I would have changed," he stammered, "if I had known, if I had guessed . . ." Kanik fluttered his hand again, for an end to the apologies, and smiled. "Clothes are not important, Ismet. But what you are here for is."

"The papers, Pasha?"

"No, Ismet. There are no papers. Pasha Demir is in trouble. He needs your help."

"Anything, Pasha. I will do anything."

"I am sure of it. And it is a simple task I ask of you. As you will know, young Pasha Mahmut is expected at Konyak today."

Ismet nodded. "His room is ready, Pasha. I have cleaned it twice most thoroughly."

"Pasha Mahmut will not be using his room. You are to meet him, Ismet, at Lusquat Airport at three o'clock. He comes by Kumarean Airways, Flight three-two-three. You are to take him with all the speed you can across the border to Nigella. There is a cave, forty miles north west of Rabass, half way up a mountain. You know the cave?"

"I know the cave, Pasha. Is Pasha Demir there?"

"I cannot tell you more, Ismet. But get the boy across the border safely." He opened the cupboard door again. "Look, take some clothes for him from here. He must be inconspicuous. How will you travel?"

"The horse and cart will do. We will hire ourselves out as load carriers. When I smear his face—and mine—we will look the part."

"It's fortunate you didn't change your clothes." Pasha Kanik's melon-slice of a smile appeared again.

"Yes, Pasha."

"Here is a little money. Not too much, for that would look suspicious. Good luck, Ismet."

"Thank you, Pasha, I will see my task through."

Flight three-two-three landed safely and on time. Ismet waited by the guarded exit point as the passengers came hurrying out, most to be greeted joyfully by relations or friends. Mahmut did not come. Ismet waited hopefully and still the boy did not appear. A military car drove off suddenly and noisily from somewhere to the side of the airport building and Ismet glimpsed it briefly through the window with growing apprehension. At last he went to the passenger desk to question an official. "Mahmut Demir?" said the official. "You are here to meet him?"

"Yes."

"He is not on the list. Wait here a moment."

The man came back with a second official who looked at Ismet, up and down. "Who are you?" he asked at last.

"I am just a servant, sent to meet young Pasha Mahmut Demir. I expected to see him come off the flight. Three-two-three I was told."

A painful silence of half a minute or so followed, and Ismet felt a prickling along his spine as the cold eyes scrutinised his face and figure.

"Well, you won't be meeting him after all," said the official coolly, at last losing interest. "Go home."

Ismet walked slowly back to the horse and cart and set out for Konyak. When he arrived he saw, as he had expected, the military guarding and observing the house. He watched for a while from the distance then, after prolonged thought, turned his horse loose and began the long, slow journey to Nigella, alone and on foot. It would be bad news that he took with him; bad and sad news for Pasha Ephraim.

General Cukurova took the report of Demir's defection with outward calm. "So!" he said. "And now Demir. You are sure of your facts, Korigos?"

"Yes, General. There can be no doubt. We were told by an electrician. He had been lying very still with some floor boards up above the Minister's office re-making a difficult connection. Through the thin plasterwork he heard a short conversation between the minister and a visitor. It sounded treasonable and he reported the facts at once to my department."

"And then?"

"A junior official took the information. I have to say that he did not believe it at first and so was slow to act."

"The official's name?"

"His name is Zeid, sir. His work is normally good. I suppose, looking at it from his point of view, it was hard to . . ."

"His point of view?" cut in Cukurova sharply. "Junior officials in the police department do not have points of view. You will punish him, Korigos—report to me when you have done so." Korigos, Chief of Political Police, brought his heels together softly and bobbed his head in acknowledgement of the order. Punishment in the greatly feared PP Squad, the general's favourite instrument of suppression, was always severe; like many who had gone before him, Zeid would have to suffer.

Cukurova spoke again: "You have other evidence against Demir?"

"We have. We searched his papers and found one small, pencilled note in the minister's writing. I have it here—perhaps you will read it." Cukurova glanced through the note, then handed it back in silence to Korigos, who continued: "Now we are searching his house at Konyak. Already many papers have come to light and it is clear that Demir has been betraying our country for several years. He has been passing information to Britain and has been planning an uprising against you. The evidence is totally incriminating."

"You have the names of his accomplices?" asked Cukurova, and Korigos noted the dangerous glitter in his leader's eyes.

"No, sir. We have not. He used code names only. We are investigating them."

"And the caller. The one the electrician heard in conversation with Demir. Who was he?"

The wretched police chief brought himself quietly to attention again, bracing for the next move. "I regret that we do not know who the caller was," he said. "He seems to have avoided the usual switchboard procedure. Nobody questioned him. But, with respect, sir, capturing Demir has the top priority, for when we have him we will learn the rest. You may be confident we . . ."

"Confident!" retorted Cukurova. "Confidence in the PPS is not always easy to maintain, Korigos. Perhaps you can understand that."

Korigos lowered his head briefly in acknowledgement of the rebuke before replying. "Indeed," he said at last. "However, I have one pleasing piece of news to report, sir. Something that means we shall certainly bring Demir into custody—and soon." He paused for effect, watching the flicker of interest that passed across the general's drawn face, then went on: "We hold his son, Mahmut. Just a boy. The two were very close. Mahmut is at school in Britain, a fact that itself may be regarded as significant. We learned from the Ministry that he was arriving at Lusquat to holiday with his father. My department moved fast, extremely fast and met the boy at the airport. He is now safely detained. This sprat will surely catch our mackerel. That is why I beg your confidence."

For a while Cukurova said nothing. Then, speaking softly, with the glitter still in his eyes he laid down his terms. "Korigos, have Demir here, before me, within five days or you will be charged with neglect of duty. We will give our former Minister a splendid trial. It can be slow and thorough this time—the world will see the fairness of it. Then there will be the hanging, a public one perhaps? We must think about that, there are arguments for and against. And of course, by then there will be others to hang, the traitorous accomplices. You must track them down, every one, and where there is doubt assume guilt. We can gain much from all this, Korigos. We can stiffen the morale of the country, destroy internal enemies and make the western powers wriggle—yes, and pay. We'll have their dollars, francs and pounds for this.

Get on with it, Korigos. Reward the loyal electrician—five hundred crowns I think—and put his story in the papers."

The police chief, more relaxed now through his leader's change of mood, brought his heels together again and began to turn to leave. Then the general spoke some parting words which brought that new and happier feeling abruptly to an end: "Korigos," he said menacingly, in little more than a whisper. "Remember. *Five days.*" Korigos looked for a moment into those cold, big, baby-like blue eyes and a new expression crossed his face as he left the room, an expression of consuming anger at the humiliation and helplessness of his position. It was not unknown for police chiefs also to dangle on the end of ropes in Kumaree.

Cukurova sent at once for the British ambassador, deliberately kept him waiting for more than half an hour in an ante-room, then received the man with a brusqueness that bordered on the insulting. "My government protests," he said, "in the strongest possible terms at the outrageous behaviour of the British government in conspiring to establish an espionage network in Kumaree, and to overthrow the lawful government of the country." He handed over a diplomatic note which said much the same thing formally and in greater detail, adding that it was assumed that Demir had defected to Britain and demanding his prompt return. As soon as the ambassador had the note in his hand, Cukurova left the room by an escape door behind his desk. The ambassador bowed to an empty room before leaving.

Next morning at ten the ambassador came back with the text of a note sent from London by cypher telegram and composed by Sir Hartley Peers and the Foreign Secretary. It informed Cukurova that the British government knew nothing of the defection of Ephraim Demir, which seemed to be a purely Kumarean affair.

At three o'clock Cukurova summoned the ambassador again and greeted him this time with a broad if chilling smile. "The time for playing games has ended," he said. "I mean to have Demir back, and I mean to have him back quickly. Inform your government that we hold his young son, Mahmut, a child of fifteen. We will use him in whatever way is necessary to secure the return of his father. The little pawn puts the king in check. Let us see what conclusions the British government draws from that." This time there was no note. The ambassador drew breath to speak but too late; Cukurova was already giving a little bow which meant that the interview was over—in less than twenty seconds.

Perry flew first and with his usual impeccable style—precise airspeed, precise height, precise courses. He was good to watch. Yankee Foxtrot seemed to be pulling specially smoothly at a hundred and fifty-five knots, the Lycomings sounding strong and steady at cruise rpm. As the minutes passed Jon began to relax, absorbed, as usual, in the joy of flight.

At twelve sixteen he saw the tall masts of Daventry

directly underneath. They looked very puny from flight level nine-zero and he studied the map intently to make a positive identification. Then Perry glanced round. "Daventry," he said, and changed course to one-seven-six for Woodley. Jon entered the time and position in the flight log strapped to his right knee and Charlie retuned the VOR receiver to one-one-four, Midhurst, a reporting point not far from the coast. The weather was being kind; patches of strato-cumulus occasionally floated by a thousand feet or so below them but most of the time they had clear, wide open skies, the midday sun glinting on Yankee Foxtrot's smart orange and white livery. They flew on, talking little but contented now in flight, with trust in each other and in Yankee Foxtrot. The VOR left/right needle remained nicely centred showing they were accurately on track.

At twelve forty-four they homed on to Midhurst, and as they crossed the beacon the "To/From" flag on the VOR dial suddenly showed "off" for "no signal received". Then, a moment or two later, as they began to leave the beacon astern, the "From" flag appeared. Charlie was watching for the sign and pressed the transmit button to call London on one-three-five decimal two-five: "London. Golf Alpha Romeo Yankee Foxtrot by Midhurst four-four. Flight level niner zero estimating Worthing at five-seven, the FIR next. Routing to Lyon." He released the button and London came back with a clipped acknowledgement, no more than the aircraft's call sign: "Romeo Yankee Foxtrot." Charlie turned the volume down until chatter between London Air Traffic Control and the inbound and outbound aircraft was just audible. They flew on in silence.

Dead on time, at twelve fifty-seven they crossed Worthing and set out over the Channel, which looked very blue and calm from nine thousand feet. Perry glanced across at Charlie and took his hands and feet off the controls, and Charlie took over without a word passing between them. Yankee Foxtrot hammered on for Lyon. In mid-Channel, Charlie called London that he was changing frequencies. Back came the swift, always courteous reply: "Romeo Yankee Foxtrot. Call Paris Airways. Good day." Charlie called Paris Flight Information Region as instructed and reported their position. The voice that answered now had a strong French accent. So it's goodbye Britain, thought Jon. They were really getting somewhere now.

Soon the Alps were in sight, the high peaks to the east looking very beautiful with their capping of snow glittering in the summer sunshine. The great green spaces of rural France slipped by below them. At fifteen twenty they began the let down to Lyon and at fifteen thirty-six, just three minutes late, Yankee Foxtrot's wheels touched the runway and they were down. Perry did the landing, the usual very pretty effort, with the tail low and the ground contact so light that it was hard to be sure it had really happened.

Charlie turned to Jonathan. "He'll be all right soon, won't he?" he joked. "Another lesson or two and we'll let him go solo. I'd say he's there." He grinned amiably at the boy and Jon smiled back. To be able to fly like that. To do it every time. To make it seem like something that just happened all by itself without fuss or calculation. "A bee-utiful landing, Perry," said Jon unnecessarily. "Bee-utiful."

Perry nodded his head in acknowledgement. "Mighty kind of you to say so, sir," he said in that slow quiet voice of his that gave few clues to the quality of the man, his speed and certainty and courage. They turned off the runway, parked and shut down the engines. It was suddenly very quiet, just the usual pleasant hum of the instrument gyros gradually slowing down and coming lower in pitch as they did so.

"Well," said Perry, "that's leg one complete. Naples next. Let's have a coffee and take a stroll to the met office." They climbed out. It was very warm and they were beginning to look sticky.

The met man was extremely cheerful. "You have no troubles with zee weathare," he said. "A liddle cumulus 'ere and per'aps zare but nutting of amportonse. Good afternoon and bon voyage."

They refuelled, wanting 88 gallons, but at 78 the bowser ran out. The attendant apologized and Charlie swore softly, but Perry took the news philosophically. "We'll settle for that," he said. "Let's go flying."

To Jon's delight they put him in the right hand seat for the Naples leg, propped up on his inflatable cushions, one underneath, the other pushed firmly down as usual against the small of his back. Charlie sat behind looking sleepy. On the climb out, at eleven hundred feet, Perry took his hands and feet off again. "You have control, Captain," he said. "Remember, we want one-five-five at nine-zero steering one-nine-zero. Okay?"

Jon nodded happily and focussed his mind to the delicate matter of flying two leading pilots to a standard they would accept. He started his usual trick of a little too much control, chasing and correcting his speed and rate of climb and course in a prolonged series of tensely made movements. Then Perry shook his leg gently with his lean, brown hand. "Relax, Jonathan," he said mildly. "Let the aeroplane fly itself a little more." The advice helped and in a few minutes everything seemed passably well under control. They levelled out again at nine thousand and before long crossed the French coast between Nice and Marseille. The Mediterranean lay beneath them, blue and exciting, Corsica dead ahead.

After twenty nine minutes Perry called for a fifty degree change of course. "Steer one-four-zero," he said. "You're doing fine. Would you like a rest?"

Jon shook his head vigorously. "No thanks. I'm okay. I'm enjoying it." Perry looked at his young face, saw that it was true, and smiled. "I'm glad we brought you along," he said. Then, turning to the rear seat, "Charlie, I guess you and I can have a sleep."

"Yeah," agreed Charlie. "But with one eye open for the fuel gauge. We're on a long leg, Perry."

"You're right about that. Five hundred and sixty-nine nautical miles."

"A bit critical, eh? Ninety-one gallons you say here on the flight plan."

"Yep. Ninety-one. It'll leave us nineteen or so—about fifty-five minutes reserve time. I'm happy with that."

"Okay. But tell the co-pilot there to stay on course. Don't get lost, Jon."

"Stop worrying, Mister Thompson," said Perry, "in fact go to sleep."

It was still hot in Naples, really hot, when they touched down after almost exactly four hours flying time, nearly all of it done by Jon; a shimmering summer's day had left the runways and taxi tracks radiating heatwaves and even now, in the middle evening, the sweat beads soon went rolling down their faces as they taxied to the fuelling point. "Let's get out, quick, and get some air," said Perry. But the outside air was hot too, and humid and abnormally still. "Well, we're getting a little practice in for Cyprus," he added philosophically. "It'll be worse there. Quite a lot worse."

"Good," said Charlie, "I like it when my shirt sticks to my back. I call that really nice. And with any luck we might get shot at, too."

Perry nodded. "We can hope. Anyway, let's get fuelled up, find some tasty pizza pie and strong coffee—and then get rolling again. Come on."

Within fifty minutes they were cleared for take off by Naples tower and were on the move. For the next leg, to Athens, Jonathan sat in the back and was glad to do so; he was dog-tired and fell asleep within a minute or two of take off. When he woke up, they were night flying. Perry and Charlie, outlined against the glowing instruments and the moonlit sky, were almost silent now, exchanging an occasional word or two about transmitter frequencies and position fixes, but there was no chat. Romeo Yankee Foxtrot was hammering along steadily at 155 knots, the Lycomings sounding very good and sure. An assortment of lights could be seen downwards, some steady and some intermittent, but whether they were ships or shoreline lights Jonathan didn't know—except for a few directly beneath; they were ships ploughing their solitary ways through the once blue, now turned black, Mediterranean. It was all very beautiful and romantic.

He watched for a while in silence, noting again the calm competence of the two Lonehead fliers. A strange pair they were, just about as different as two men could be. The lean, dark, soft talking, good humoured Perry, a man with a mid-Atlantic drawl of a voice, an American-born European-based man who came nearer to being truly international than anybody else Jonno had ever met, and whose charm had every girl dreaming of ways to make him settle down at last—with her; and the bulky, moody Charlie Thompson with his ragged red moustache, big hands and unpredictable moods, his rash moments and strong sense of fair play; his all round lumpiness, as Roz often called it. Different, yes, but when it came to flying, these two were as one, skilled and cool, utterly on top of the job.

"How long 'til we get to Athens?" Jonathan asked at length.

Charlie turned round. "Aha, so you're with us again, are you Captain? We're almost there, mate. About half an hour to go. We've been cleared to land already and we're losing height to three thousand at five hundred feet a minute. Perry is conducting the orchestra and doing a satisfactory job."

"You seem to have managed all right without me!" complained Jon.

"It wasn't easy," Charlie said, gravely. "But we got by."

As they approached the circuit the Athens controller, a girl with an alluring Greek accent, called them. "Golf Alpha Romeo Yankee Foxtrot call on one-two-one decimal four."

Charlie was about to answer until Perry raised a restraining finger. "Thanks, Charles, but I'll have this pleasure. Remember who's captain." And he pressed the transmit button. "Yankee Foxtrot. Changing to one-two-one decimal four." He glanced a shade impatiently across at Charlie. "Go on, then. Change it." And Charlie with a disdainful shrug retuned.

Perry transmitted again. "Athens approach, Yankee Foxtrot calling on one-two-one decimal four."

Back came the pleasant Greek voice. "Yankee Foxtrot. What are the names of your captain and others on board?"

"Yankee Foxtrot. Captain is Peregrene Langhorne. Others on board are Charles Thompson and Jonathan Kane. We wish to land and refuel en route to Akrotiri."

"Yankee Foxtrot. What are the ranks of all on board?"

"Athens Yankee Foxtrot. This is a civilian aircraft. We do not repeat do not have military ranks."

"Yankee Foxtrot. Stand by," she said. And a pause followed.

Perry looked round at the other two. "A good deal of notice seems to be being taken of our arrival."

"Does it matter?" asked Charlie.

"I'm not sure. Maybe we should have filed the flight plan for Nicosia, the civilian airport, instead of Akrotiri. I think they're suspicious. Think we're military or something."

"Well, change the plan now. Call them."

Perry pressed the button again: "Athens approach. Yankee Foxtrot. Correction to my last message. We are en route for Nicosia. Negative Akrotiri, affirmative Nicosia. Do you copy?"

"Yankee Foxtrot. Understood. You are cleared to land on runway three-three. QFE niner-niner-eight."

"Yankee Foxtrot. Three-three. Niner-niner-eight. Thank you." Perry muttered to himself: "She's got the voice of a Greek angel—but I don't much like it. I hope she isn't going to be more like a Trojan horse."

"Eh?" said Charlie.

"Let's get the gear and flaps down. Do the approach calls for me."

They dropped towards the floodlit runway and a welcome that sounded uncertain. As usual the wheels touched with the gentleness of a caress.

Jonathan felt the tingle of excitement again. Charlie seemed to feel it too. "It's a funny thing," he murmured, "but the further east you go the dodgier it gets."

A polite army major spoke to them in the tower. "You seem to be in some doubt about your destination, Captain Langhorne," he said.

"Well, sir, we're ah, not . . . The way I see it, is this," mumbled Perry. "We'd like to file for . . ." and then the major, smiling a little, interrupted him.

"We had a telephone call from RAF Akrotiri asking for news of you and requesting us to give you our best assistance. We expected a military aircraft. In any case we are happy to oblige."

"Oh, yes. I see." Perry was relieved. So there wasn't going to be trouble after all. "Well, that's very kind of you. Yes, it's Akrotiri we're bound for."

"What can we provide you with?"

Perry's eyes had focussed beyond the friendly major towards a girl, a very beautiful, slender, sunbrowned girl who was looking candidly back towards him. The major glanced across and the smile shrank briefly to around half its former size. Charlie noticed the eyes game too, and nudged Perry's arm. "We have to be in Akrotiri in three and a half hours," he said in an urgent undertone. "The whole of the Near

East Air Force Command of the Royal Air Force awaits us. Remember?"

The major continued: "We can offer fuel, food, coffee and the weather picture, Captain."

"Thanks. We could use them all. What's the weather at Akrotiri, actual and expected?"

"Good, and continuing good. No problems."

"Great. We'll try to be away in half an hour or so. We'd be glad to take you up on that coffee, and I guess Jonathan would like a Coke." The girl walked away, disappearing through an inner door and out of Perry's mind.

"Come with me, please," said the amiable major. "As you say in England, have it on the house."

Soon after take-off the sun started to rise, pushing slowly up past the edge of the world, and Jonathan, once more in the back, watched the magic of a Mediterranean dawn with, minute by minute, the brilliance of summer daylight taking over from the darkness, and the blue coming back to the sea and the silver to Yankee Foxtrot's wings. This, he decided, was living; really living. Something to tell them at school next term. Or, on second thoughts, maybe not. That might lead to other boys making offers of help to Perry. No point in inviting unnecessary competition. An island lay behind them with a yellow and silver shoreline. He tried to match the island's shape to the map. Crete perhaps. He leaned forward between the two front seats. "When do we get there?" he asked. "To Cyprus?"

Perry answered. "Six o'clock their time. Put your watch on an hour if you haven't done it yet." He was looking a bit tired now; so was Charlie. There was very little talk between them.

At five forty Charlie reached for the VHF tuning knob. "I'll try giving them a call on one-two-two decimal one," he said, and Perry nodded.

"Akrotiri. Aztec Golf Alpha Romeo Yankee Foxtrot. Do you read?"

Akrotiri approach control came back immediately. "Yankee Foxtrot. Reading you four. Go ahead." Charlie stuck his thumb up in the air triumphantly, then transmitted again.

"Yankee Foxtrot. Approaching you on one-zero-four at flight level niner-zero. Estimated arrival Akrotiri zero two. Request landing instructions."

The Akrotiri controller was courteous and efficient. "Yankee Foxtrot. Radar identified. You are cleared to descend to two thousand. QFE one-zero-zero-four. Runway one-one. Left hand. Call again this frequency when you have the field in sight. You will be clear for a straight-in approach."

Jon tapped Perry's shoulder and pointed left. "Look!" he yelled. Two glittering Lightnings, sleek and dangerous, were flying in tight formation a quarter of a mile or so to the left. They streaked away ahead into the distance. "Crikey," he went on, impressed. "Where's the fire?"

"It's not that," said Charlie. "It's just that we're going backwards."

"That'll be 56 squadron," murmured Perry.

"That's nothing for them. You see how they go when they bang on the re-heat. Wouch!"

Soon the vast sprawl of Akrotiri airport was visible ahead and they were cleared number one to land on one-one. "Go on, Charlie," said Perry. "You take her in this time. Show the RAF how to do it." And Charlie did exactly that. It was another greaser as smooth as featherdown. "Super!" said Jonathan approvingly as the roll slowed down. They were directed by the tower to leave the runway at an intersection to the right, then to follow a car to the parking point. Charlie pulled the mixture control levers fully back and the throbbing Lycomings stopped. The engine nacelles were streaked with oil. Perry hung his headset on the control wheel. "I'm kind of tired of sitting down," he said, "and tired of engine noise. Come on, let's get out and have a look at Akrotiri."

As they dropped off the wing to the ground, they found a squadron leader standing by to greet them. He saluted informally, then shook hands. "My name is Patterson," he said. "Duty Officer. I have to take you to the station commander's offices. There's quite a reception committee waiting for you." He opened the car doors. "Will you all hop in, please?"

"More sitting down," grumbled Perry, and Patterson drove them past glittering aluminium hangars, towards the administration centre a low, white building with a red tiled roof. "Yes," muttered Charlie. "And Fenwick Wotsisname on our backs already. To hell with him! I want a beer and a nap—just an hour or two with my head down."

"You know something Charlie?" said Perry: "You won't get either. I've a hunch the action is about to start. Have a look round the world—just in case you're not to be part of it much longer." Charlie looked up sharply for a moment and then out across the strangely white soil of Cyprus and the scrubby trees.

"But I'm too young, pure and beautiful to die," he said.

Chapter Four

DO NOTHING RASH

"Then we are agreed," said Henry Wright mildly. "One hundred hand-woven carpets at twenty-five lira, the quality to be as good in every case as this sample. When will they come?"

"Soon, Effendi. Soon. Perhaps two weeks." The white robed Nigellan smiled broadly and held out his hand. "Let us seal our transaction with a handshake. It is work and food for many people. There will be rejoicing tonight."

"Good, but not too much noise I hope," answered Henry, shaking hands. "I can't stand noise, you know. Hate it. Hate it!"

"No noise, Effendi. Just a rejoicing in the hearts. And now I will take the good news to my band of weavers. And so . . ." he bowed ". . . until two weeks. Good day, Effendi, and may the heavens bless you and your house."

"Yes, yes. Thank you. Good day to you."

Wright, a pink faced, grey haired man in immaculate white trousers and sweat shirt folded the sample carpet, tucked it away into a corner of the stonewalled room and wrote a note at an old-fashioned, stand-up desk: "25L. 100 carpets. See sample. Two weeks." He dated it, tucked it under a blotting pad and then pulled another paper from his pocket and smoothed it out. This, a telex print-out, was addressed to Henry Wright, Principal, Anglo-Nigellan Trading Company, and carried a heading, WORLD COMMODITY PRICES. Rows of figures followed. Opening the lid of the desk he took out a battered copy of Oliver Twist and placed it beside the prices list. His left index finger moved across the printed figures, pausing at each third and fifth entry. The third figure directed him to a page in the book which he found with his right hand; the fifth figure indicated a particular word on the page or, if it had the abbreviation 'max' alongside it, to an individual letter. On a scrap of paper he slowly, laboriously wrote out this message:

"Demir discovered has fled son believed captured but require confirmation request you find facts give help reply three one seven."

Henry was still pondering the significance of the message when a manservant appeared from a room behind the shop. "Mister Wright will eat now?" he asked.

"No, Hakki. Not now. I will be out for the rest of the day. Mind the shop for me, please." He put the old book away, calmly rolled up the scrap of paper into a twisted spill, lit it with a gas lighter, then used the spill to light a cigar. As he stepped out into the sunny, dusty street, he flicked the burning remnants of the spill away and saw the ashes start to disintegrate in the hot summer breeze. He climbed into a Range Rover parked on a nearby plot where an old building had collapsed years ago and been left as rubble, and started up. Slowly and carefully he drove through the small, narrow, Moorish-looking township and out onto the network of potholes Nigellans called a road.

Henry Wright, always a shy man and now almost a recluse, shunning the company of other people since his beautiful Nigellan wife and six-year-old daughter had died in an air crash twenty-two months before, was well known and, in his own peculiar way, respected by the simple, open-hearted townsfolk of Rabass. There were less than a dozen motor vehicles in the town and Wright's dust-covered Range Rover was instantly recognised as he made his way through the market place before turning north, and many people waved as he passed. But soon he was alone, clear of the settlement and clattering over the axle-breaking potholes. A party of eight or nine people including children, all seated on plodding camels, came towards him several miles out in the open scrubland and Wright, to avoid disturbing them, slowed down. The women modestly pulled white veils across their faces as they passed him, but the men and children smiled and nodded their darkly weathered heads. A wandering family of camel breeders, he decided, living by their wits and, no doubt, often by stealing from the already impoverished farmers. Well, life was like that for some in this forgotten corner of the world and who was he to criticise? He accelerated away again towards the Kumarean border.

About an hour later the track twisted through a gaunt outcrop of rocks and he steered the Range Rover carefully between the sharp, unyielding edges. Then, beyond the rocks, the next stretch of track reached far ahead, thin and straight like a pointer to infinity, quivering in the heat. It was lonely out here; like being at sea in the tropics, far out and alone in a little boat. As he picked up speed, he glimpsed a figure just discernible in the distance. The figure disappeared a moment later and curiously, failed to re-appear. Wright watched expectantly as the distance closed but there was nothing more to see. An odd occurrence; odd merely to meet a solitary person so far from a village but more so when the figure takes to cover.

As he neared the spot where the man had been, Henry groped under the seat and brought out a plastic bag. He tipped it upside down on the seat beside him to the right, and a Beretta thirty-eight fell out. With practiced fingers he slipped the safety catch to "off". Over to the left was a slight depression in the scrubland fringed by a stunted carob tree and other shrubs. He stopped the car some yards before the spot and scanned the silent scene with half shut eyes. "Come out!" he called at last. "I can see you." In fact he could not. Nothing was visible but the scrubby vegetation and heavy stones.

"Come out," he called again. "Come out and I

won't harm you, but if you don't I'll shoot. That's my last warning. Come out *now.*" Then, after a pause, he put the Beretta out through the window and fired a single shot towards the sky. The crack of the explosion sang uncomfortably in his ears; more noise—the hated noise. But the plan worked. A figure dressed in peasant's clothes came slowly out from hiding and towards the Rover.

Henry put the gun down and stepped from the car. "I'm Henry Wright," he said. "A trader from Rabass. Who are you and why do you hide?"

Ismet stood for a moment in silence as he comprehended his incredible luck, a faintly ridiculous looking figure dressed in a cheap, open-necked white shirt, coarse black trousers and peaked cloth cap. He was covered in dust and sweat; you could see the grime clogged in his drooping moustache. "God is with me, Effendi," he said, taking off his cap and tucking it under his arm. "It is you I am journeying to see. My name is Ismet."

"You are on your way to me? What for?"

"My master needs help. Pasha Demir, Minister of the Interior. He has fled and hides now in a cave. You know the cave?"

"I know it all right. I'm driving to it now. Get into the car. You look tired."

"Being tired is not a problem but the thirst is difficult to bear." Ismet walked slowly round and settled himself in the car. Henry handed him a plastic cup and filled it with water from a bottle. The tired, ageing servant closed his eyes and drank the water slowly, luxuriating in the pleasure of each swallow.

"Thank you, Effendi. I am fully restored."

"I'll drive slowly on, Ismet. Tell me everything you know."

"My master believes that the dictator, Cukurova, is guiding our country to the east—into the hands of communist powers. I do not pretend to understand Pasha Demir—I only know he is a good man. It is his life's wish to see the Kumarean people free. He looks towards the west, to America, to Britain, to France. The great democracies. It is important, he says, to be free to disagree."

"As you say, he is a good man, Ismet."

"They call him a traitor."

"We know who the traitor is. What is the position about Mr Demir's son?"

"Ah. Bay Mahmut. The news of him is bad. The soldiers took him from the airport. That is all I know."

"When?"

"The day before yesterday, as he arrived to spend his holidays at his father's house in Konyak. Pasha Demir asked me to meet him and take him safely to the cave. Alas, I failed."

The track was even worse out here, a swathe of hard-rimmed potholes and volcanic stones that shook and rattled the car, jarred the two men uncomfortably and punished the tyres. But Henry drove determinedly onwards at about twenty miles an hour towards the border land, a long wake of dust lying behind them and drifting eastwards in the wind.

"Tell me the rest, Ismet. You have just come from the cave?"

"Yes, Effendi. I lay a whole day near the border. I dared not cross until dark. The sun shone all day. It was a furnace."

Henry nodded sympathetically. "An uncomfortable day for you, Ismet. But later you crossed without being seen?"

"Yes. That part was not difficult. I found the cave before dawn. Pasha Demir was there."

"How did he take the news about Mahmut?"

"Not well. He was distressed. He says he must return to Kumaree and give himself up in return for Mahmut's release."

"But he is still at the cave?"

"Yes, Effendi. He sent me to find you. I rested until ten then set out expecting to arrive in Rabass at perhaps eleven o'clock tonight. For a man of my years the walk is long. He said he would wait three days. Then, if I have not returned and you have not made contact, he says he will surrender to the guardpost on the Kumarean border. He believes Cukurova would release the boy."

"How old is Mahmut?"

"Fifteen."

Henry pondered for a moment then replied. "Yes," he said, "the General would set him free —why not? But the price is too high. A very great deal too high. Tell me, Demir—Mr Demir—is in good health?"

Ismet made a wry expression and hunched his

shoulders uncertainly. "Physically he is fit. But his mind . . . He paces about the cave like a hunting lion. He is greatly troubled." They drove on in silence.

Fifty minutes or so after picking up Ismet, Henry turned the tortured Range Rover off the track and drove slowly towards a valley that passed between strange, white limestone cliffs. The afternoon sun reflected off the rock face with dazzling brilliance and Henry had to drive between the towering walls with his eyes half closed. Some freak action of weather and time had carved a tunnel-like shaft far into the vertical face at one point and Henry turned in here and stopped, plunged now into sudden darkness. He turned the headlights on and waited a minute for his eyes to adjust. "I daren't take the car any further," he explained. "We'll leave it in here, a bit further down. I'm afraid you've got some more walking to do, Ismet. All right?"

"All right, Effendi."

The car began to move again, the headlights flashing off brilliant facets of the rock and leaving eerie black shadows in the hollows. Three hundred yards or so along the tunnel, Henry switched off the engine and lights, put on a white, linen jacket, placed the Beretta in the right hand jacket pocket, slung some binoculars round his neck and climbed out. Ismet followed.

They walked back to the entrance, paused again in this strange world of contrasts, then stepped from the blackness of the tunnel into the dazzling sunshine. Turning left they made their way slowly and in silence along the base of the cliff, Henry leading. After a while he stopped and pointed up the cliff face. "It is not so steep here. Can you climb it?"

Ismet, already stiff from his days of walking, looked apprehensively up the white wall to its top where it seemed to meet and touch the scintillating blueness of the sky. "I cannot do it, Effendi. I am not a young man."

"Then we must go round. Three miles further on, the ground rises on to the plateau. We'll have to come back along the cliff top again so it will take time. And we'll have to be careful—I've seen soldiers there before now. Come on." So the painful, plodding effort began once more.

When they reached the high ground Henry, from behind the protection of a rock, scanned the scene ahead and to the sides through his binoculars, then beckoned Ismet to keep moving. Ismet, very lame by now, struggled gamely on. There were no soldiers to worry about today.

At nearly seven o'clock they arrived close to Demir's hiding place. Henry had been to the cave before but even so he found it difficult to find and Ismet, fatigued to the point where he was mentally confused, was not much help. At last, pushing through some more of the dried-up, scrubby bushes, they found the entrance and Henry called out. "Demir, Demir! Can you hear me? It's Henry Wright. I'm here with Ismet."

A moment later Ephraim Demir stepped out. "Thank God!" he said as the two men shook hands.

"You've been quick. Come into the cave."

Henry helped Ismet through the entrance. "Your servant is done in," he explained. "He needs a very long rest—twelve hours, perhaps more."

"Poor Ismet," said Demir, putting a hand on the loyal servant's shoulder. "You have done well." They made him comfortable in the far point of the cave where, after swallowing a cup of tepid soup, Ismet at once fell into an exhausted sleep.

"I will make you some coffee," Demir said. "And we must talk. You will already know that that swine Cukurova has my son. I am prepared to die to have him freed."

"Do nothing rash. We need time to think. D'you know where your boy is being held?"

"Almost certainly at Akarya prison. That's where the maximum security prisoners go."

"Well, the situation is clear. We must get him out mustn't we?"

"It's impossible. Impossible!" Demir was starting to pace about again.

Henry raised a single, expressive eyebrow. "Impossible? That is a word I seldom use. Are you going to make the coffee?"

"Yes, yes. I'm sorry." Demir lit a camping stove and put the coffee on. It was soon ready and he poured the black, bitter liquid into mugs.

Henry, sitting on a camper's folding chair, managed to look comfortable and at ease. He sipped his coffee thoughtfully. "I am in touch with Whitehall, Demir. They know the position and we must give them time. You have supplies enough to hold out here for several weeks. I beg you to be patient."

"I should not have come."

"I think you should. And, anyway, you have. So see it through."

As Henry left a little over an hour later, he threw a packet to Demir. "Take one of those. It will help you to sleep. And I'll be back soon—within two days I hope. Au revoir." He slipped out of the cave entrance, made his way rapidly to the plateau, deftly climbed down the crumbling cliff face and retraced his steps along the valley to the tunnel entrance. It was after nine o'clock and the sun was setting now, leaving a streaked red and purple sky behind. At the entrance to the tunnel before moving into the darkness, he took the Beretta from his pocket and moved the safety catch to "off". A gun at the ready helped even if you couldn't see to use it to any real effect.

Just inside the entrance Henry heard a movement and froze, pressing back against the rock face. A moment later something floundered over his feet brushing roughly against his legs and raced for the entrance. He hardly saw it as it flashed round the corner and vanished but it hadn't been anything much; a goat perhaps. He shook his head in mild reproof at what he felt had been a silly over-reaction, then put the gun back in his pocket and walked briskly to the car.

He arrived back in Rabass at about eleven-thirty and went at once to the telex machine in the little office behind the shop.

With the help of the well-thumbed Oliver Twist, book, he tapped out a message to London: "Have seen Demir at cave confirm son captured Demir suggests he surrender immediate action London indicated am standing by Wright."

Henry put the book away, wandered into the simple kitchen that Hakki kept as clean and polished as an old ship's engine—and yawned. It had been a tiring time. He made himself some cocoa, took it to bed and fell deeply asleep with the drink untouched.

Chapter Five

MOMENT OF DECISION

Squadron Leader Patterson tapped on a door marked "Station Commander" and walked through, beckoning to the others to follow. "Molly, I've got Peregrene Langhorne and his crew," he said to a good looking WRAF officer who rose to meet them. "The Oscar Mike affair. Is the Air Commodore ready to see us?"

The girl opened an inner door, put her head round it briefly, murmured something inaudible to Perry and the others, then opened it wide and stood back. "Will you please all go in?" she said. A wiry, spry little man in civilian clothes sprang from a chair and hurried over to greet them smiling broadly and showing large, irregular teeth. "Delighted, delighted," he said. "Now, you'll be Mr Langhorne. So glad you've arrived. I do hope you had a good trip over." He held out a hand which Perry dutifully shook. "Now let me do some introductions. I'm Fenwick (he pronounced it Fennick) Pinkerton of the MoD—er, Ministry of Defence. This is the Station Commander over here, Air Commodore J. C. Dow-Smith." He gestured towards a big, amiable-looking grey haired man sitting behind a vast leather topped desk, who now stood up and shook hands. "Glad to have you at Akrotiri," he said. "If there's anything you need, any of you—" he glanced round at them all "—you've only to mention it to me."

"Thank you," murmured Perry. "We won't forget."

"Now," went on Pinkerton, "I would like you to meet Mr Refet Yalman." Again Perry shook hands, this time with a man everybody looked at twice. He was physically quite small but had a look of sinewy strength about him, and there was something about his face. His hair was black and short, and he wore a neatly trimmed moustache, also black. His eyes, dark brown and vivid, flicked restlessly right and left and gave the feeling that they saw beyond the surface of things. Clearly this was a man of intelligence, of sharpness; and a man in a hurry. His voice had the sort of cutting edge you would expect from his appearance. "Günaydin," he said. Then, with a momentary smile, "Good morning." Perry nodded and murmured a "Good morning" in return.

The spry man, Pinkerton, was going on again. "Now Refet—I'm sure he won't mind if we get on first name terms—Refet is a Kumarean and does good work for us. Very good work indeed. Ah yes, but let me introduce the others."

Charlie and Jonathan had been standing awkwardly near the door and Pinkerton beckoned them forward. "Air Commodore, this is Mr Thompson I believe and, with him, Mr—eh, Master, heh heh, well, Jonathan Kane. The Station Commander shook hands and Jonathan noticed the broad blue band of rank on his sleeve, and the medal ribbons including the DFC that he wore above his left pocket, and the RAF wings just above the colourful ribbons. Despite all this, the man had a friendly, informal manner and a handshake strong enough to hurt. "I didn't know we were recruiting men so young," he said, smiling, "but you look good aircrew material to me. What's your rôle in the operation?"

"He doesn't have any," said Charlie quickly, protectively. "He's going for a swim."

But Refet Yalman's quick eyes had noticed Jonathan and weighed him up. "I'm not so sure," he said. "Perhaps there *is* a rôle for him."

Charlie, the man of moods, the former child from a broken home, Charlie the good friend, glowered across the room at Yalman and drew breath to speak. But Pinkerton of the Ministry of Defence fluttered his hands and spoke first. "Now, let's all sit down and I'll put you in the, um, picture." They sat, and the spry little man went on. "First, are you all covered by the Official Secrets Act? Have you all signed the form?"

"Yes," said Peregrene.

"Including the boy?"

"Sure. Why not?"

"Yes, yes. Of course. Quite so. Well, what we are doing here is top secret. I really must warn you that if you talk about it to outsiders, even accidentally, the consequences may be very serious for you."

Perry frowned. "I don't like threats," he said. "Nor, to be frank, do I like the whole goddam' situation we're getting into."

The Station Commander leaned forward, shaking his head briefly. "Pinkerton doesn't mean it as a threat," he said. "It really is his duty to impress on you the seriousness of what's happening. There's one hell of a lot at stake on this operation. We've got to get it right and we've got to keep it quiet."

Perry's lips went rather thin and firm and there was silence for a moment. Then the crisis was past. "Okay," he said. "Let's get on with it."

"I think you know what the object of the exercise—Operation Midnight as we call it—is. We have to fly a British contact, Ephraim Demir, out of Nigella where he is in hiding. And I think you know that there is a complication, namely that his son, Mahmut, has been arrested and held in Kumaree. We have just had a signal from London that Demir will not accept sanctuary from the west unless his boy can be got out too. Thus, um, a relatively simple operation has become difficult." Fenwick Pinkerton paused for effect and it was clear he was enjoying his rôle of proclaimer of the plan. "However," he went on, "we shall overcome the difficulty. All difficulties. I have complete confidence." He smiled toothily at them, one by one, and Perry lowered his eyes to examine the floor.

"Now, we have not been tardy at the MoD and the FO. The present position and future proposals are . . ."

The Air Commodore came to the rescue. "Pinkerton," he said quietly, "I suggest you let Mr Yalman tell his latest news, keeping it brief, and that Mr Langhorne and his friends then have some breakfast and a sleep. They look tired to me. Let's cut it short."

The Pinkerton smile shrank for a moment then came back. "Of course, Air Commodore," he said, and turned to the dark-eyed man. "Refet, tell them, will you, what you've found out?"

Yalman folded his arms across his chest and leaned forward intensely. His piercing eyes were focussed most of the time on Jon, still reading the boy's tired face and searching, it seemed, for answers to questions he hadn't put. He spoke quickly, almost impatiently and smiled a lot, but it was a little smile that came and then went again with curious suddenness. "Already I know which prison Mahmut is in," he said. "And even which cell he is in. And most important of all, I know how to get him out." The vivid eyes flicked round the room looking briefly at his audience, man by man, assessing the effect of these dramatic words, then locked again onto Jonathan. Perry's face had turned expressionless, Charlie frowned, Pinkerton beamed and the station commander studied a little loose skin on the index finger of his right hand.

Yalman continued: "He's in Akarya jail, the east block, cell seventeen. Now that is the cell for important solitaries. It has its own little exercise yard and it's closer to the outer wall than the other cells. With the help of someone who's physically smaller than a grown man but who has a man's heart, I can get Mahmut out. I know exactly how to do it."

Charlie's frown had deepened. "If you're thinking of using Jonathan, think again," he said gruffly. "He's going swimming."

Yalman got up and began to pace about the room. "You're quite right," he said. "I *am* thinking of Jonathan. I had the whole rescue figured out, but there was one missing link. It needed a boy, an absolutely dependable, intelligent, determined boy"—Yalman pointed now at Jonathan—"like him. And I didn't know of *any* boy who could be trusted. Then in you walk with Jonathan. I would call it providential."

"And I'd call it barmy," said Charlie. "Forget it. Let's have plan two."

Peregrene nodded. "Charlie's right," he said. "I'm sorry but the question of using Jon just doesn't arise. He's only here for the ride."

"Well, what do you say, Jonathan?" Yalman put the question directly now, his eyes locked on the boy's face again.

Charlie bounded to his feet, a big-framed craggy figure impressive in his anger. "Cut it out, Yalman," he said. "You've already been told the kid's not in this. Any plan that depends on somebody his age won't do. Think of something else."

Pinkerton began to flutter again. "Gentlemen, gentlemen, do keep calm," he urged. "Let's all be constructive. I'm sure Refet would never allow the boy to come to harm."

"Look," said Perry. "We seem to be reading the

end of this story before the beginning. Yalman, how do you know so much about Mahmut—cell seventeen and all that? You've been quick."

"I'm always quick. You'll learn that. Well, I can't tell you everything but I live near Akarya and have my contacts. I make a point of keeping in touch with the goings on at the jail. A very useful thing to do at Kumaree, I do assure you. It's just a matter of knowing the right people, a gift here and there, a favour or two. You understand, I'm sure. Besides, I'm a builder. I repaired a rotten floor in the governor's office about a year ago. Oh yes, I'm quite well known."

"You seem a funny kind of a sport to me," said Peregrene candidly. "What's *your* angle anyway? Why get involved? Good grief, why are *any* of us involved?"

Yalman took on a certain dignity when he answered. "Kumaree is my country. Like Ephraim Demir, the great and steadfast Ephraim, I want to see it free. I want to see Cukurova's grip ended—broken, smashed. That's my 'angle' as you put it."

"Okay. And this information you've got. It's right? You're absolutely sure?"

"Absolutely sure."

"Let's hear the plan then. Only perhaps you'll keep it short. As the Air Commodore said, we're goddam' tired."

Yalman waggled his head, a jerky up and down movement of comprehension. "I understand. Well now, prisoners in cell seventeen are lucky. As I said, they have a little exercise yard of their own. It's very small, about nine metres by seven, and the walls round it go many storeys high, but the good thing is they can use it any time they like. There's a door to the yard in the cell itself. They can wander in and out as they choose."

"And you are suggesting Mahmut might wander up the wall?"

Yalman ignored the sarcasm. "No, Mr Langhorne, I am not. That would not be feasible for several reasons—including an electrified fence round the top."

"So it's a tunnel?"

"Not exactly. The floor of the yard is concrete, about two metres thick and reinforced with steel mesh. I wouldn't like to have to tunnel through that."

"Let's have it then."

"A hundred years or so BC, the Romans came to my country. They left many fine buildings—and a drainage system. Some of their pipes are still in use, including one that carries rainwater away from the little courtyard. Now Roman pipes are big. This one is forty-five centimetres at its narrowest part—big enough for Jonathan to climb through."

The anger showed on Charlie's face again. "Rubbish!" he said. "Jonathan isn't climbing through a sewage pipe for anyone."

"It's not a sewage pipe. It's a stormwater drain only. Surely you can imagine how a little enclosed courtyard like that would flood when the heavy rains come if there weren't good drainage. There is no other outflow to the pipe. The authorities don't want to drown their distinguished prisoners you see—at least not while they've still got a use for them."

Charlie, unmollified, was starting to speak again but Perry overrode him. "What's the size of the outlet?" he asked. "I mean the grating in the floor of the yard?"

"About forty-five centimetres, like the pipe. Only square."

"Fantastic!" protested Charlie. "Even Cukurova can't be that stupid. You're telling us that with all this top security going on he goes and leaves a way out like that? Does it light up at night?"

Yalman's vivid eyes flashed with sudden anger but he controlled himself and answered civilly. "No," he said, "there are no illuminations. The grating is considered to be escape proof. It is a massive piece of cast iron tied immovably into the concrete. I doubt whether even a pneumatic drill would shift it a millimetre." He stopped talking for several seconds and moved towards the end of the room. There he turned to face them all, leaned back against the door and folded his arms tightly across his chest again—the Yalman signal of something important about to happen. "So, you are asking yourselves, what *will* move the grating? And I have the answer. A thermic lance. The latest thermic equipment will cut through the iron like the proverbial knife through butter."

"Don't tell me," said Charlie. "Just don't tell me. We're to airlift it in. We'll find an armour-plated helicopter and drop the thermic lance to Mahmut with a bar of chocolate and bullet proof pants. It can't fail."

Pinkerton looked imploringly towards Perry who threw a little disapproving wave at Charlie. "Cool it a bit, Charlie, will you?" he said. "The man's entitled to a hearing."

"Yeah, I'm sorry. But Jonathan's not going anywhere rougher than the beach. Is he?"

"I guess he isn't. But just hear it out." Charlie slumped dejectedly in his chair and seemed to switch off, gazing idly through the window. Pinkerton, visibly happier, smiled and nodded to Yalman. "Carry on, will you, Refet? Um, yes—please carry on."

"Well, somebody, somebody of Jonathan's size, goes into the pipe from the outlet end pushing the lance in front of him. When he gets to the grating he cuts through from underneath. Within fifteen minutes Mahmut would be free."

Perry glanced at Jonathan, then at the ceiling, then back to Yalman. "You have the thermic gear?" he asked.

"I know where to get it."

"It's light enough for a boy to handle?"

"Yes."

"And simple to operate?"

"Yes, quite simple. And I'd give him a bit of practice first."

"Are you sure Jonathan can get through the pipe?"

Yalman picked up a ruler from the Air Commodore's desk, walked over to Jonathan and turned him round. "Put your hands up in the air, please," he said. When Jonathan did so, Yalman measured across his shoulders. "Thirty-five centimetres," he said. "No problem."

"No problem?" queried Perry. "Isn't that on the tight side?"

"He's got his clothes on. Stripped to the waist he'll go through like a mole."

"How does he get into the pipe at the outer end?"

"That's easy. The pipe ends in a huge soakaway. I'll go down in my contractor's van to make some improvements to the whole outfall arrangement—and believe me there's room for improvements. Jonathan will be my apprentice. I'll dress him up in the right sort of clothes—the simple stuff the peasant children wear. It will all look quite natural. Nothing suspicious. Then we'll put him in the pipe in the early evening. He'll have to wait for an hour or so—until it's really dark. Then he wriggles up, and that's that."

"What about Mahmut? He's older than Jonathan."

"Yes, but he's very thin. We have his vital statistics—there's no problem there either."

Perry turned to Jonathan. "You've been very quiet," he said. "What's going on in that head of yours?"

Charlie hunched forward and glared towards Peregrene. "He's wondering what the water's like," he muttered. "And whether the jelly fish here sting."

Jonathan had gone rather pink in the face as the roomful of eyes turned to study him. "I . . . I'd like to do it," he murmured. "And I think I probably could."

The Air Commodore got up from his desk, walked over and put a hand on Jonathan's head. "You're a good chap," he said. "And a brave one. I hope you'll join the Air Force someday. But before we get you involved in Operation Midnight, we'll have to speak to your father. Mr Pinkerton will assist with that —later." Then, speaking to them all, he brought the meeting to an end. "For the moment, let's break it up," he said. "Our visitors can talk things over among themselves and have a good long rest. I'd be glad if you'd all join me for drinks at six this evening."

Patterson drove them to the officers' mess for breakfast, then to a two-bedroom transit officers' apartment. By some sort of natural law, Perry had a bedroom to himself and the others shared. Charlie had another go at Jon just before they went to sleep. "I don't want you involved in this," he said sourly. "Keep out of it, mate."

"Well, anyway, I've got to speak to my dad," replied Jonathan. "I wonder how? Long distance telephone I suppose. D'you think they'll scramble it?"

"I've no idea. But you talk to your dad. He'll tell them where to put their Operation Midnight. Now get some sleep." They slept well.

Perry woke them at about three in the afternoon with the news that Pinkerton was in the flat. "He wants a little talk," he explained. "So come on, you guys—I can't face him alone."

Despite the summer Cyprus heat, Pinkerton was looking very fresh and civil-servant-ish, smartly clad in a dark-coloured, lightweight suit, immaculate white shirt and club tie, and smelling fragrant from scented talcum powder or after-shave lotion—or maybe both. He greeted them in the little sitting room with nods of the head, the toothy smile and an expressed hope that they had all slept well and felt refreshed. Already, he explained, he had cypher-cabled Sir Hartley in London who had replied stressing the British government's anxiety about the possibility that Demir would surrender. The key to it all, Sir Hartley had signalled, was speed. "So, gentlemen," he went on, "as the bard almost said, 'stand not upon the order of our going'. Heh heh. Shakespeare."

Charlie was scowling again. "Did you mention the kid's part in all this?" he asked.

Jonathan, suddenly angry, glanced coldly across at him. "I don't like being called a kid," he said.

"Sorry, mate." Charlie understood and softened for the moment. "No offence meant." Then, rounding on the dapper Pinkerton again, "Well, did you?"

"Oh, um, yes. He sees nothing wrong with it providing the father is consulted."

Charlie looked furious again and his ragged ginger moustache seemed to stick out like a porcupine's spikes. "Then when we get back," he said, "Sir Hartley Thing's got a slap on the snout coming. From me!"

Peregrene raised a quietening hand. "Charlie," he said, "cut it out! Relax. I'm pretty sure Jonathan won't be going—but it's up to his parents and himself. Just let it go, and calm down." Pinkerton, looking relieved, left soon after to place a telephone call to Jonathan's house, which he hoped would come through at six-fifteen. There was a moment of awkwardness after he'd gone, then Charlie, the man of moods, put on a small, rather forced grin. "Sorry, Perry," he said.

"Forget it."

"There's a Mirage Three parked out there. A visitor I suppose. I'll just go and ask the crew chief if I can have a look round it." He ambled from the room.

Perry, sitting on the arm of a service-issue easy chair, took the chance of a private word with Jonathan. "Tell me, Jonno," he said in that soft, attentive, drawly voice that was a built-in part of the personality of the man, "Tell me, what do you *think* your father will say?"

"I'm pretty sure he'd say 'all right'. Leave it to me, sort of thing. But I don't think my mother will agree. She'll probably make him stop me."

"I kind of hope she does. But if they do say Yes, how do you feel about the job? D'you want to do it?"

"It's not exactly that I want to; it's that I wouldn't feel quite right if I didn't. As if I'd funked it. You know."

"Sure I know. I think we see things the same way. We should never have got into this in the first place but since we *are* in it, we'd better try to see the job through. Look, Jonno, if you do go, there's something you must take with you. I'll show you now." He flipped open his overnight bag and pointed to a zipped-up canvas package the size of a shoe box.

"What's that?"

"A personal survival kit. Something you can carry in your haversack. Unzip it and have a look."

Jonathan unzipped and gently tipped the contents onto the floor. A small pocket pistol came out first. "That's a Beretta point thirty-eight and it's loaded," explained Perry. "Eight rounds. Don't expect it to knock down a house—but at short ranges you could have a good friend there."

"And what's this?" Jonathan was peering now at two box-like metal objects linked together by an electrical wire; one was yellow, and the other green and yellow. The green and yellow one had the letters SARBE and "Transistor Beacon" written on the side.

"That's a SARBE—rhymes with Derby. In other words, Search And Rescue Beacon Equipment. It sends out a repeating radio bleep on two-four-three megahertz—that's the international emergency frequency. If anything goes wrong and you're on the run from Cukurova and his merry men it could be one hell of a big help when we go looking for you."

"How d'you work it?"

"It's easy. Like this." And Perry explained. At the finish they packed the SARBE and Beretta back in the bag and zipped it up. As they closed the suitcase again, Perry gave a quiet little laugh. "Now, when your dad says No, which no doubt he will, you can forget all about it—but that SARBE's quite a toy, isn't it?"

"It's really great."

Charlie came back soon after, chatting about the French Mirage—"a very pretty aeroplane", he called it—and later they walked across to the Station Commander's office for the six o'clock party together, stepping out from the comparative coolness of the flat to face a still blazing sun and hot air shimmerings that made the buildings seem to dance.

Pinkerton and Yalman were already there holding drinks, an iced gin and tonic for Pinkerton and a dark red wine for Yalman. Perry asked for rye whisky, Charlie for beer and Jonathan for a large iced Pepsi.

Air Commodore Dow-Smith poured himself a Scotch and held it up. "Well," he said, "at least we're independent thinkers; every man a different drink! Here's to your health and the success of Operation Midnight." They raised their glasses and drank the toast.

By six-thirty, Pinkerton was fluttering about the room looking anxious behind the usual toothy smiles. Telephone contact with England had still not been made and the operator rang through to report trouble on the lines.

"We must just be patient," said the Station Commander philosophically. "Let's run over the plan—we'll assume we spring Mahmut somehow. Pinkerton, spell it out please."

"Yes, yes, Air Commodore." The little man's pleasure at being asked showed in everything about him. With quick, nervous movements, he unfolded a map on the desk and Perry, Charlie and the Air Commodore gathered round to study it. "Now, gentlemen, it's really frightfully simple," Pinkerton said. "But of course that's good. Nothing like simplicity—you should have asked Napoleon about that one, heh heh." The Station Commander made a throat-clearing noise and Pinkerton hurried on. "As soon as Mahmut is over the Kumarean/Nigellan border to join his father in the cave, our contact in Rabass, um, yes, we're all bound by the Secrets Act so I can say that that's Henry Wright, well, he informs us of the fact. Mr Langhorne and Mr Thompson then make a landing under cover of darkness here . . ." he placed an immaculate finger on the map . . . "and pick him up. Ah, the two of them up. Tactically, it's all very easy. The, um, flying part is a little more difficult though, heh heh. Right, Mr Langhorne?"

Perry ignored the question but began drumming his fingers. "We've got eleven hundred feet to roll, Charlie boy," he said, "then a ninety foot rock dead ahead on climb-out. And we'll be four up! Let's fuel Yankee Foxtrot up with dynamite."

A lengthy talk began then on how to make the pick-up and survive. Yalman took no part in it and his eyes flickered across to Jonathan over and over again. With the others deeply engrossed, he walked across to the boy and whispered in his ear. "I have something important to say to you—alone. Please announce that you're still tired and would like to have another rest. Please."

For a moment Jonathan looked uncertain about what he would do, then whispered back, "All right." Yalman winked, patted him lightly on the hip and walked away.

"Perry, I'm still a bit tired. If nobody minds I think I'll go back to bed for a while."

"Sure. Okay. If the 'phone call comes through you'll have to run back."

"I'll go over with him," said Yalman. "I want my cigars anyway—I left them in the mess. See you later, Air Commodore. Thanks for the drink."

Outside Yalman became very earnest and intense. "Jonathan, I trust you," he said. "And I need you, need your help. Kumaree needs you. Your own country needs you. The men, women and children under the yoke of Cukurova need you. For all of them, for free peoples and oppressed peoples, I want to ask you to do something." His sharp eyes flickered searchingly towards Jonathan's face. "Will you do it?"

"Do what?" Jonathan's heart had begun to knock.

"I'm sure you know. And it's a big thing." Yalman paused and they walked on slowly towards the mess. "I want you to come with me now. We must get Mahmut out, *must* get him out. Don't wait for the 'phone call. The answer might be No. So come now. Slip away with me to Kumaree. I swear we will be successful, and I beg for your help. *Will you do it?*"

Despite the still high temperature of the evening an unpleasant chill had spread through Jonathan's inner self and his cheeks had turned pale. Yalman walked on with his head twisted sideways and his restless brown eyes searching through the boy, reading his thoughts and passing him strength.

Jonathan stammered a little as he replied. "You . . . you mean just us, just the . . . the two of us go off to Kumaree? And we don't tell Perry?"

"Yes. Exactly that. Then in forty-eight hours we'll have Mahmut in the cave re-united with Ephraim, his father. And you'll have gone down in history. It's not a difficult thing we have to do. We just drive to Nicosia Airport and fly out as tourists to Akarya. There's a service car here for my use and I've a van parked at Lusquat, the airport for Akarya. You know the rest. Trust me Jonathan, and say you'll do it. *Now.*"

Jonathan's heart was knocking harder than ever and he felt a throbbing in his ears. "All right," he whispered. "I'll do it."

The quick smile came to Yalman's lips, then went again. "You make me feel proud." He seemed quite emotional as he spoke the words. "You're a very gallant boy, Jonathan. Well, no, I won't call you a boy any longer. You're a man in my eyes now. Look, the car is over there. Let's just hop in and go."

"I'll get my haversack. I won't be a moment." Jonathan tried to run towards the flat but his legs wouldn't do it. They'd gone strangely stiff and wouldn't run. He tried to make them again and again and then, with his heart still knocking and ears throbbing, he walked awkwardly to the flat. He put a sweater and socks in the haversack and noticed that his fingers were trembling. Then he began to feel sick and sat down for a few seconds on the bed. He remembered some advice Perry had given him about fear. Stand still, he'd said, stick your head up high and breathe in deeply ten or a dozen times. He tried it but the truth is it didn't seem to help very much; perhaps a little. He took Perry's zip-up bag and put it in the haversack too, and a bar of chocolate he found lying on the table. Then he left the coolness and safety of the flat and walked stiffly towards Yalman's car.

Moments later they drove out of the airport, pausing to show passes to the sentry, then set out for Nicosia. A fairish drive, seventy miles at least. Yalman drove very fast, rocking and sliding round corners and pushing hectically through en route villages, tooting the horn and slamming up and down through the gears. The excitement of the drive helped Jon to forget the overpowering fear that had gripped him earlier, which was something on the good side. But about eighty-five minutes after leaving Akrotiri when they flashed past a sign saying "Cyprus International Airport", Yalman slowed down and the fear came back. "We've made it," Yalman said. "There's a Cyprus Airways Trident due off in twenty minutes and we'll be on it."

When they stepped from the car Jonathan had great trouble with his legs again. But there wasn't a minute to waste. Like a pair of hurried tourists they made it through the ticket hall routine and across the apron, Yalman looking confident and businesslike and Jonathan still feeling sick but moving at a fast hobble, and they caught the plane.

At nine forty-five p.m. the three Rolls Royce Speys started up and, as the big jet taxied out, Yalman patted Jonathan comfortingly on the knee. "That's the worst part over," he promised. "You'll see."

Jonathan tried to reply but had trouble now with his vocal chords and, worse, his eyes were going wet. He managed a nod, then turned to the window and hoped Refet Yalman would leave him alone for a minute.

Yalman seemed to understand, and did so.

At home, an unusually agitated Sir Hartley Peers travelled by chauffeur-driven car to the Kane's house in a pleasant part of Burton-on-Trent. He arrived at just after ten, British time—eleven in Cyprus and Kumaree—at the same moment as Jonathan and Yalman were on the approach to land in the Trident Three at Lusquat Airport, nearly two thousand five hundred miles away. Sir Hartley's job was to apologise, a function he frequently had to perform in his rôle of senior diplomat. On this occasion he felt more deeply about his task than usual.

Roz had gone to the house, too, and in the sitting room the four of them, Mr and Mrs Kane, Roz and Sir Hartley sat down with cups of coffee to discuss Jon's sudden disappearance from Akrotiri. It had been a distressing evening for Mrs Kane; the call *had* come through from the RAF base in the end, and she *had* refused to allow her son to go with Yalman. He's so young, she had said. Too young. There must be another way. Then, soon after, there had been the other call, this one from Whitehall, passing the news that Jonathan had gone anyway, as far as could be judged, quite freely and on his own decision, and could not be called back; the Private Secretary to the Secretary of State, she was told, was on his way to explain.

"I'm so sorry, my dear lady," Sir Hartley said in his misleadingly mild voice. "And for security reasons I cannot go into details. But the department and I do express our most sincere regret. In, ah, thirty years of service I've never known us slip so badly on a banana skin before."

Roz looked across at him coldly. "I think it's disgraceful," she said. "Deplorable." Then she turned to console Mrs Kane who was squeezing and re-squeezing a handkerchief in tensely clenched hands.

Henry Kane was calmer about it all. "Well, Jonathan's gone," he said. "And that's that. I don't think we need to talk as if he were dead. He's pretty good at looking after himself, and we must just hope for the best. Thank you for coming, Sir Hartley. We mustn't detain you too long."

A few minutes later Sir Hartley, grateful for the release, left to return to London. He repeated his regrets and gave an assurance that every effort to trace and return Jonathan safely would be made. "And, ah, um, one other thing," he added. "The matter is still secret. Not a word, please, to anyone. *Anyone.*"

Outside he knocked on the roof of the Ministry

limousine to wake the chauffeur up, turned to beam a smile of farewell towards the Kanes and Roz, stepped into the car and was gone.

On the way back, he composed a new note to Cukurova. In it he acknowledged a recent furious and threatening message from the general and replied, very bland as ever, that "Her Majesty's Government continued to regard the defection and disappearance of Ephraim Demir as a purely Kumarean matter". He "regretted his department was unable to help".

General Cukurova received and read the message at eight o'clock the next morning. At nine o'clock, Korigos, Chief of Political Police, was hanged a hundred feet or so away from Mahmut's cell.

Chapter Six

YOU'RE ON YOUR OWN

At Lusquat Airport, Yalman presented papers to two sets of officials and spoke briefly in Kumarean, gesturing from time to time towards Jonathan. Whatever he said seemed satisfactory and they were allowed through.

They passed through the airport building and out to a very dark night beyond it. Yalman pointed ahead and spoke quietly into Jonathan's ear. "My van is parked over there. Keep silent until we are in it." They walked on. There had been a shower, a heavy one, that had left many puddles and strange contrasts of reflected airport lights and dark shadows. It took a good ten minutes to reach the van, an old uncared-for looking Chevrolet.

Once inside, Yalman turned to Jonathan and smiled. "Now we can relax," he said. "So far so good, eh?"

"Yes."

"Now, there will be times when I must speak to you in Kumarean. Try to look as if you understand. If I look at you questioningly and nod my head up and down, answer 'Evet'. That is 'Yes'. If I shake my head sideways reply, 'Hayir', meaning 'No'. Is that clear?"

"Yes."

"Good. Now we will drive to Bin Eski. He is also working for the cause." At first the van wouldn't start but Yalman persevered, looking anxiously round and about from time to time, and suddenly the engine clanked noisily into life. They drove six miles or so and drew up at a shop-like building with a yard beside it. There were various mounds in the yard —sand, building stones, untidy piles of scaffold tubes and other builder's bricabrac. "Follow me," said Yalman, and they walked through the yard to a side door. Yalman unlocked the door and they went in. The building smelled stale and felt damp. Yalman switched on a feeble light and they made their way upstairs.

On the first floor they found a heavy man asleep on a badly sagging bed. Yalman shook him roughly. "Saat kacta uyandirmami istiyorsunuz?" he said. "When would you like me to wake you, eh? Saat dokuzu ongece? At ten past nine?" He laughed as the other man opened his eyes and levered himself into a sitting position.

"Look," Yalman went on, "this is Jonathan, a young friend of ours. We must talk English for the sake of our new friend." But they didn't. They chattered away in rapid Kumarean and the only words Jonathan understood was his own name which came out now and again. He sat down on a battered wooden chair, noticed that the feeling of sickness had come back—and waited. He would have given ten years of his life to be anywhere but here in this strange, dim, damp, comfortless, oppressive house.

At last Yalman beckoned him to another room and pointed to a mattress on the floor. "It is gone one o'clock," he said. "Rest there. Tomorrow is the big day. Bin has done his work well and all the equipment is ready. In the morning there will be a lesson for you in how to use it. Then we go to the outfall end of the discharge pipe and begin our building operations. And after dark, frisssh! we have Mahmut out."

Jonathan lay down tensely. His mind wandered back to all he had left behind. He thought of his parents, of Roz and her sparkling eyes, of Lonehead field, of the little Pup, of Peregrene and Charlie; it was another world they all belonged to. A few hours passed without sleep and, soon after dawn, Yalman re-appeared in the room carrying a bundle. He looked as fresh and quick as ever but his clothes had changed. The well-pressed suit had gone and in its place was an open-necked check shirt and coarse black trousers. Jonathan noticed the start of a black stubble on his chin which gave him an altogether rougher appearance. But the flickering eyes were the same, and the hurried movements. He smiled at the expression on the boy's face. "I look a little different, eh? So will you. Get those fancy pants off and put this on." He threw the bundle onto the mattress. Jonathan gazed at two crude garments, a shirt and trousers, lying beside him. "I can't wear these," he said.

"Put them on."

"But they . . . they look dirty. And, anyway, they're much too big."

"Put them on. Roll the trousers up a bit. Come downstairs when you're ready." Yalman walked from the room. Miserably, Jon got into the grotesque garments and made his way downstairs where he found Yalman in a workshop drinking strong black coffee and examining a clutter of equipment. "This is the thermic lance," said Yalman. "It's surprisingly simple for what it can do."

Lying at his feet was a thin steel tube about ten feet long screwed into another, shorter tube with a valve-like tap in it. The length of the whole thing must have been fourteen feet at least. Leading from the shorter tube was a high pressure flexible hose—like the air line at a service station; it lay in a tangle of coils and was connected to a heavy steel cylinder painted blue.

Yalman pointed to the longer tube. "That's the lance," he said. "It's the business end of the gadget. And this"—he pointed now to the other tube-like object—"is the lance holder. See, it has a valve. When you open the valve, pure oxygen flows along the lance and over lots of little steel rods lying inside. When you heat the end of the lance, right on the tip, and let the oxygen flow you get the best firework you've ever seen—believe me. Don't worry about *why*, but the lance starts to burn at a tremendous temperature—three to four thousand degrees Celsius.

Push it up against concrete or steel—or other materials you wouldn't expect to burn—and you just bash right through it."

Jonathan looked doubtfully at the crude equipment. "Have I got to drag that all the way up the drain?" he asked.

"Not the oxygen cylinder. Just the lance and connecting tube. You'll manage it."

"What about smoke? How do I breathe?"

"You'll be wearing a mask, but in any case you'll find there's quite a draught blowing through from the exposed outfall end. You'll feel it pass over your body and on up through the grating to carry the smoke and fumes away. It's all been thought of. See? So don't worry. Come on. I'll show you how to light the lance." They dragged the steel tube out into the yard, heated the top with a portable oxy-acetylene cutter and the promised firework display took place.

During the latter part of the morning they loaded the thermic lance equipment into the van and, afterwards, Yalman and Bin Eski sat down to a hurried meal. They ate something unrecognisable to Jon who, in any case, wasn't hungry. There was more talk in Kumarean, a bit one sided since Eski didn't do much more than grunt, then Yalman turned to Jon and said, "We're about to go. Hop into the van." Jonathan went back to the mattress, stuffed his London-style shirt and trousers into Perry's zip-up bag and walked out with it to the van. In a way he felt glad that the moment for action had come. The sooner the show began, the sooner it all would end

—one way or another.

Eski didn't come, but stood at the door as Yalman started up the van and moved off. It took them only twenty minutes or so to drive to the outfall. The big pipe poked out from rising ground and, after heavy rain, released its water onto a large circle of loose stones forming a soakaway. At present everything was very dry and hot. Between two and three hundred metres away, on up the slope, stood the grim, fortress-like building of Akarya jail. The outfall stood on the outskirts of the town which lay beyond the jail, sprawling across several square miles.

Jon studied the pipe uneasily for a while. "It's going to be a very long crawl," he said. "I . . . I hope I can do it." But Yalman, who was unloading spades, picks, a large hold-all of tools and a workman's tent ignored the remark. "Help me get the tent up," he ordered. "That's where we'll store the gear." Close to the pipe outfall they erected the tent, a simple affair of steel tubes and canvas.

"Now take your shirt off," Yalman said. "And get busy. We're going to have to do some real work." Stripped to the waist, and with sweat rolling off them, they began lifting the heavy stones and stacking them to one side. Beneath the stones lay rubble through which the stormwater was supposed to filter and disperse. The debris of many years had washed down below the stones to make an almost impervious layer blanketing the rubble and reducing its efficiency. Yalman obviously knew what he was about, and they began forking out the rubbish carefully and throwing it to the side.

Jonathan tired after no more than an hour and sat down for a rest on one of the bigger stones. "Keep at it," commanded Yalman. "Somebody's coming."

A man in uniform came quite slowly towards them from the direction of the prison and Yalman turned to meet him at the critical moment, smiling broadly. The two men spoke together briefly, then Yalman produced a paper from his hip pocket which the uniformed man studied, and handed back. More conversation followed, and the uniformed man began laughing at Jonathan and said something unintelligible towards him. Yalman joined in the laughter and also spoke in rapid Kumarean to the boy. Jonathan, increasingly frantic at so much attention being directed towards him, noticed that Yalman's head was giving little up and down nods and he groped in his mind for the word he should speak. Yes, he remembered now. "Evet," he muttered—and there was renewed laughter.

The man stayed a minute or two longer, then strolled back towards the jail. "I don't think they'll bother us again," said Yalman. "We'll take a break now for a drink. By the way, a man was hanged in there this morning."

"Hanged—what for?"

"In Kumaree it doesn't have to be for anything. Come on, let's have a rest. Then back to work."

They sat for a little while in the shade of the van and drank tepid water from a flask Yalman had brought. One good thing about all the physical effort and the heat and the coarse, chafing trousers was that most of the time they kept Jonathan's mind off the dangers lying ahead. The feeling of sickness had gone, giving way to assorted aches and discomforts that were, on the whole, more endurable. He put the shirt on again to protect his shoulders from the sun.

They worked on, though increasingly slowly and with a number of short breaks, through the afternoon and early evening. At one point, after a careful look round, they carried the gear from the van and placed it in the tent, all out of sight. Then the forking out and heaving about the place of stones continued. Yalman took a watch from his trouser pocket quite often but each time put it back without comment until, suddenly, he announced that the time to stop had come. "It's seven o'clock," he said. "If we go on any longer it might look suspicious."

"If we go on any longer, I think I'll just fall over," replied Jon. "I'm done in. I really am. And my back and hands hurt."

"Get in to the back of the van and I'll tell you what happens now." There was something about Yalman's face as he spoke that sent the fear rushing back into Jonathan's inner self. The man's lips had gone very thin, very pale, and his voice had quietened almost to a whisper. Jonathan's heart began to thump and bang away again and he had the same old difficulty with his legs as he walked round the van and climbed in through the loading doors in the back of it. Yalman followed him in and closed the doors so that for a moment they were in darkness. Then

Yalman switched on a low-powered torch that was lying on the floor and a little bit of vision came back.

"You'll have to get into the drainpipe now and wait there for darkness. I'll take the van away and walk back later."

At first Jonathan hardly comprehended what was being said. But soon the message got through. "You *can't* leave me alone," he said in a quieter whisper even than Yalman's. "It won't be dark for hours yet."

"I've got to leave you. It's the only way."

"But I can go too, and walk back with you."

"No you can't. You'll be almost naked. Take your shirt and trousers off—I'm going to grease you with this." He took the lid off a foul-smelling tin.

"Please don't. I can't do it. I'll be sick." Jonathan was pleading now, beside himself with horror. "Let me stay with you."

"The van might be searched, anything could happen. I don't want you hanging around. Now come on." Yalman pulled at the loose fitting peasant shirt and it came straight off. "Stand still," he said. "And stop being a baby." Jonathan trembled violently in his trunks as the stinking animal fat was spread over his arms and legs and torso. Yalman put the lid back on the tin and cautiously opened one of the doors. It was good to see the light streaming in again. "Wait there," he whispered. "I'll make sure we're all clear."

He came back in a minute with some of the tools and threw them into the van. "Come on then," he said, sounding almost casual now. "Out you get

—and straight into the pipe."

Jonathan clambered down and dragged himself bare-footed across the stones and into the pipe outfall with his hands stretched out ahead of him. Coolly, Yalman continued to walk about picking up a few hand tools, tidying a stack of stones that looked unstable, and securing the tent. As he passed the pipe he said, "Go further up. I can see your feet. And don't in *any* circumstances come out. I'll be back after dark." There were some more clatterings of tools being thrown about near the van and then the engine started up. Jonathan listened as the creaky old Chevrolet clanked away into the distance. Resting the side of his face on the coldness of the ancient Roman pipe, he gave way to a great surge of feeling and allowed the tears to flow. "Stop being a baby," Yalman had said to him cruelly. Well, he was crying like one now. At least there was no one to see, no one would know; so there was that much to be said for being alone.

After a while he steadied up and the crying stopped. Then came bitter moments of anger at his own weakness and, after that, a new determination to do what had to be done and to do it well. He had got himself into this situation and he would damn' well see it through at whatever cost. A strange calmness settled over his mind and he lay very still, waiting. Nothing moved or stirred. There was a curious feeling of disembodiment, a detachment from time, an unreality about the silence and containment. It seemed strange, very strange, that a few yards up the blackness of the pipe were men enduring the many miseries of Akarya jail—among them, of course, young Mahmut. They would be talking, swearing, weeping, above all suffering. Yet here, in the pipe, aloneness was everything. A world complete by being nothing. Nothing.

A sudden splash of light began to dance in the pipe and he heard Yalman's voice from the outfall end. "I'm back. Come out a minute. Quick!"

Jonathan eased himself out to see a starlit sky and the familiar face of Yalman who held a flashlight, now switched off, and who was looking less composed than usual. "I've had a difficult time," Yalman said. "There seem to be soldiers, police, jailers everywhere tonight and they're full of curiousity—so I'm going to hand you in the cutting gear and disappear again quickly. You get on with the job by yourself. I'll be back in about an hour for you and Mahmut. When you've finished just wait inside the pipe down at this end until I give you a call. Then come out. Is that all clear?

"I suppose so, yes. Couldn't you hide in the tent?"

"What if somebody looks inside it? They might."

"In that case we're done anyway—aren't we?"

"Wear these." Yalman cut off the conversation by pulling a goggled facemask over Jonathan's head and handing him a pair of heavy duty gloves which he put on. Almost naked, but gloved, goggled and greased, the boy looked as if he'd just dropped in from Mars. Yalman was too hurried to see the joke and handed across the flashlight. "And take this," he said, "and this"—the portable oxy-acetylene cutter. "And get moving."

In some ways the drainpipe seemed more terrible lit up by the torch than it had in darkness. Cold, tomb-like, blackened by the grime of centuries, it seemed to stretch into the distance for ever. Jon felt the long, awkward thermic lance being pushed up beside him, and took hold of it. Then Yalman was half calling, half whispering some last words. "Be quick, and good luck. You're on your own." So he was shoving off; all very well for him. Jonathan couldn't think of any suitable reply and said nothing. The slow, uncomfortable wriggle up the pipe, pushing and pulling the torch and cutting gear with him, began.

At moments he had the hideous feeling that the pipe was closing in on him, gripping and choking him; and then a flash of pure panic would race through to his mind overwhelming and possessing it absolutely and all but paralysing his ability to move, and setting the cold sweat flowing and his heart hammering. The fight back for control took everything the boy could find in his inner self to win. But each time he did win, and then the fear would subside freeing his muscles for action again and allowing the forward push to continue.

Soon his knees and elbows began to hurt from the scraping they were getting against the Roman concrete. With difficulty he twisted onto his back and managed a few yards like that; then over onto his front again; and on, and on. The flexible hose became harder and harder to pull as the distance increased and the animal fat, which didn't seem to be doing anything for the rest of his body, got onto his hands and made them slip when he tugged at the thermic lance. Cursing and panting, he struggled on and arrived at the prison end at last. He lay still for some moments, resting.

The upper half of the drainpipe was above ground level and the lower half below it so that the grating was L shaped, partly built into the massive wall and partly flush with the ground. After his short rest, Jonathan wriggled up, put his forehead against the vertical part of the grating and peered through. Very dimly in the starlight, the little courtyard could be seen. There was still no sound, no movement—just this same bleak sense of desertion. So what now?

Jonathan switched on the torch and had a quick, careful look at the grating. It was a very strong looking affair indeed, and he understood the need for a thermic lance. Only modern equipment like that had a hope of getting through. He switched the light out again. Before starting work he supposed he'd better try to rouse Mahmut to explain. Mahmut might be rather surprised to wake up and find a private firework display going on in his exercise yard. Jonathan took the mask half off, cupped his hands round his mouth and called Mahmut's name in a husky whisper through the grating. "Mahmut!" No reply. "Mahmut." Pause. "Mahmut—can you hear me? Mahmut! I've come to get you out. Mahmut!" And at last there was a movement in the courtyard and Mahmut was standing there, tense and hesitant.

"I'm over here, by the grating. Don't be afraid. I've come to get you out through here. We're going to take you to your father."

Mahmut walked over and crouched down by the grating and Jon shone the torch on him. He saw a thin, dark-skinned, anxious youth wearing spectacles peering back into the blackness of the pipe. "Who . . . who are you?" Mahmut asked.

"I'm a boy. Jonathan Kane. I'll cut this grating away, then you can wriggle down the drainpipe with me. It's a good job you're thin! I've got to use a flame to cut through the grating—a thermic lance, you know, the thing bank robbers use. Is there anybody about—a guard or anyone?"

"No. They leave me alone at night."

"All right. I can't explain any more for the moment. Stand back, I'm going to light up." He lit the oxy-acetylene cutter and played the bright blue flame on the end of the lance. When the tip of the lance had reached white heat he wriggled quickly back down the pipe a few feet and turned on the gas flow. Immediately, a dazzling spurt of flame jetted out and vivid sparks began to fly. Yalman had been right; it was some firework. Backing still further down the drainpipe and away from the flame and smoke Jonathan put the super heated tip of the lance against the grating. Now the display of fireworks grew even more spectacular. Smoke made it difficult to see where the grating was being burnt—but it didn't appear to matter. The lance just consumed anything it touched and made the massive grating burn like paper. In less than two minutes the heavy ironwork had gone, leaving a jagged, smoking hole. Jonathan turned off the flow of oxygen and the flame died away. With relief he pulled the mask off his head and called out again to Mahmut. "Are you still there?"

"Yes."

"Well, give it ten minutes to cool off, then come feet first into the pipe. Take your clothes off."

"Clothes off?"

"Yes. Go on. Roll them into a ball and bring them behind you. I'll help pull you through by your feet if you stick."

For Jonathan, the journey back down the pipe was a positive pleasure. For one thing, the pipe sloped downwards gently so gravity made the wriggling easier. But what really mattered was that the job was done, and successfully. Mahmut was out, free.

All that remained now was to avoid getting caught at the getaway stage—and that was up to Yalman. The two boys forced their way down the drainpipe, pushing the clutter of equipment before them and dragging Mahmut's clothes behind. They made good time but had just arrived at the outfall end when Yalman was calling for them in that strained whisper of his. "Jonathan. Are you there?"

"Yes".

"You've got Mahmut?"

"Yes."

"Come on out then. It's all clear. Hurry!"

They crawled out into the cool, sweet night air

and, without explanation Yalman began to lead them down the slope and away, Mahmut carrying his clothes. "What are we going to do about the cutting equipment?" asked Jonathan.

"Leave it. We'll call it a present for General Cukurova."

Mahmut, tottering along like Jonathan in bare feet, was looking bewildered. "If you don't mind, sir," he said politely, "I'd like to put my clothes on."

"Later. In the van. I want to get away from here fast." Obediently and often painfully, the boys struggled along on their bare feet.

The van had been parked beside a disused building, Yalman's theory being that it was safer to leave it there, where it seemed to belong, than out in the open where it would look conspicuous.

"You two get in the back and clean yourselves up a bit," he said. "Then I want you to hide until we're over the border. There's an old tarpaulin in there—get under it. I'll stop in a couple of miles to see that you're properly covered up. Go on." They clambered into the back and a moment later the old engine began to clank again and the van moved slowly away.

Jonathan shone the flashlight over himself and was astonished at the sight. Dirt from the drainpipe had stuck in large amounts to the animal fat so that he was grotesquely dirty from head to toes; he was grazed in a dozen places and a trickle of blood was coming from his right knee. "Good grief!" he said. "What a mess. And I stink, too."

"I'd better be honest about it," said Mahmut in

the quietly modulated tones of an expensive English private school. "You do! You smell terrible." And they laughed together.

With some old rags they rubbed as much of the grease off Jonathan as they could and tied a grubby piece of cloth round his injured knee. Then they dressed—Jonathan still in the coarse peasant's shirt and trousers—and crawled under the tarpaulin. Yalman made his inspection soon after and seemed satisfied. "The main danger is at the border," he said. "When we're safely through you can come into the front." He went back to the driving seat and the van began to creak and rumble again along the rough Kumarean roads.

The two boys lay flat on their backs and talked. Jonathan explained the background to the rescue and explained how he'd slipped away alone with Yalman, leaving Perry, Charlie and the others behind at Akrotiri.

"That took some guts," said Mahmut appreciately. "I doubt if I could have done it."

"Of course you could. It wasn't too bad."

"So now we're on our way to meet up with my father?"

"That's the idea. He's in a cave somewhere. We all get together, then Perry flies us out in the Aztec. He's a super pilot—he really is just about the greatest."

Another half hour or so passed and the van came to a stop. Yalman talked to someone for a while through the window, then got out and the back doors of the van were opened. There was more talk in Kumarean, and Yalman gave a little laugh. The doors closed again and Mahmut turned to whisper in Jonathan's ear. "The frontier guard, or whoever he was, was talking about the smell in here. He didn't like it, I'm glad to say. Thanks."

The van began to roll again and a few minutes later stopped for the boys to move into the front. Jonathan sat between the other two. "It shouldn't take very long to reach the cave, should it?" he asked. "Two hours perhaps?"

"Longer than that," replied Yalman. "I can't risk the direct route."

"I thought we were safe now."

"Saf*er*. But a Nigellan bullet makes just the same hole in you as a Kumarean one. Don't worry, though. I know what I'm doing. About four hours should see us through."

Mahmut spoke next. "I'm very grateful to you, sir," he said. "You've been taking big risks for my father and me." Yalman gave a brief nod of his head, and drove on in silence.

Dawn came up soon after the encounter with the guard, and the day grew rapidly hotter. "Another scorcher I'm afraid," said Jonathan as the sweat began to gather on his face. "Is there a ventilation fan anywhere?"

"The fan doesn't work. You'll just have to put up with it." They drove on in discomfort without further talk.

The terrain began to change, becoming very sparse and desert-like, and then changed again, dramatically, as they climbed a twisting track of a road that took them to higher altitudes and cooler temperatures. They arrived in time at a wild and lonely area of rocky outcrops, cones, pyramids and needles formed by water erosion working on hardened volcanic lava. A mysterious mist hung about in some of the hollows and gave the scene an air of ghostly unreality.

The van stopped at last beside an obelisk-like rock. "See that?" said Yalman. "Hermits hollowed out rocks like this in ancient times and lived in them. You'd have to look a long way to find a better hiding place, wouldn't you?"

"Is this where my father is?" asked Mahmut with quickening interest.

"You'll see. Just a minute."

Almost at once a man stepped out of the rock and walked over to Yalman's side of the van. "Gosh," said Jonathan. "It's Mr Eski. How did *he* get here?"

Eski looked as solid and bear-like as ever. "I see you got him," he said, nodding towards Mahmut. "Good."

"Yes, the plan worked well." Then, turning to Jonathan and Mahmut, "Come in to the hideaway."

They climbed up ten roughly cut steps and in through an opening in the wall of the rock, Mahmut going first, Jonathan following and the two men coming in behind them. The boys examined the half-dark interior, a bare, rock-floored chamber, but there was no sign of Ephraim.

Mahmut turned round, a questioning expression

on his face. "Where's my father then?" he asked. Eski appeared at that moment, from behind Yalman, and he was holding a heavy shotgun pointed towards the boys. Yalman did the speaking. "Sit down," he said. "On the floor—both of you. Your father isn't here. Bin, put the iron socks on them."

Jonathan went into a state of dry-mouthed shock, and his heart began to bang and thump as the truth broke through a momentary numbness of the mind. So, all that he had gone through had led to this; to some sort of unbelievable double-cross—and more danger and misery.

The misery began fast. Eskie dragged a heavy ball and chain of the kind used on slaves years ago and clamped it on Mahmut, pulling his right shoe and sock off and locking the cold bracelet round his ankle. Then he brought another over and fixed it to Jonathan. Mahmut had turned pale but seemed very calm and even dignified despite one bare foot and the ball and chain. Gazing level-eyed through his black rimmed spectacles, he spoke a word or two to Yalman. "Bu iyiliginizi hic unutmiyacagim," he said, bowing slightly. Then, turning to Jonathan, he explained, "I have just said that I won't forget his kindness."

The little darting smile that had so often come to Yalman's face had gone for the moment. "You may have reason enough not to forget," he replied. "Reason enough."

Jonathan tried to speak, found his tongue and lips difficult to control, then managed a rush of questions, his voice sounding strained and husky. "Why have you done this? Why . . . why are you holding us? What's it for?"

Eski appeared with two folding canvas chairs and both men sat down facing the boys on the floor. They had all grown accustomed to the half light and Jonathan, gazing into the flickering eyes of Yalman, caught a glitter there, a coldness and cruelty he'd never seen before. He felt helpless and afraid.

"I don't mind telling you why you're here," said Yalman. "It's because I want Ephraim Demir, our illustrious Minister of the Interior. He's a greatly wanted man, that father of yours, Mahmut. Cukurova wants him. The western powers want him. And I want him. And I'm the one who's going to get him."

"I don't think I understand." Mahmut spoke calmly. "You mean you're not acting for Cukurova?"

Yalman flicked on that tricky smile. "Of course not. I'm working for me—and for Kumaree, oh yes, for Kumaree. Cukurova is corrupt, grossly corrupt; and he has many enemies. I'll soon blow the screens away from him. With the information I'll twist out of Ephraim I'll have the general running, and then this nation will be great again, with me at its head."

"My father wasn't able to do it."

"Your father is a fool."

"Fool or not, he won't fall for your ridiculous trap."

"I think he will, Mahmut, I think he will. D'you remember that little Kumarean sport of ours called falaka?"

"I know what you mean."

"Jonathan, you won't have heard of it so I'll explain. We beat the soles of your feet until the flesh comes away. That's all. And you scream, and we tape your screams, and we send the tape to Ephraim who comes to us. As fast as he can get here, I imagine."

"And then what?" asked Mahmut. "You kill him?"

"No. Not for a while at least. Later, who can say?"

Mahmut glanced across at the pallid, strained face of the younger boy, and managed a smile. "We're in the hands of madmen, Jonathan," he said. "What's more, I'm almost certain we're still in Kumaree—I've seen this place from the air. Bad luck, isn't it? But try not to worry. We'll just do what they want for the present."

"Yes, they're mad," replied Jonathan, with his tongue and lips under better control now. "They must be mad. But we can take it can't we? Whatever's coming to us." He took a few more of Perry's long, deep breaths and this time they seemed to help a little.

Chapter Seven

WE'LL PUT UP ANYTHING

Peregrene woke to find Charlie standing in the bedroom gazing out through the window. He was already dressed in his sweatshirt and baggy slacks. His free-growing reddish hair was in greater disarray than usual, standing up from his head in a tangle of spikes and layers, and his broad shoulders were hunched forward. Those hands, small hams of hands, were hooked by the thumbs into the seams of his trouser pockets straining the stitches to breaking point. Even viewed from behind, Charlie Thompson was a picture of unease.

"Morning, Charles," said Perry, and Charlie turned abruptly round.

"Perry, it's now thirty-six hours since Jonno went missing. We've got to do something."

"Yeah."

"And wait 'til I see Pinkerton today."

"He's keeping out of your way."

"So he should. I'll kick his ass for him."

"Yeah. Do. And you could water his beer."

A flash of anger showed on Charlie's face and gave

his moustache that curious starched-fibres look again. "Perry, I'm not joking. We've got to get the kid back."

"Yeah. I don't think it's funny either. And Charlie, sir, I think getting Jonny back is going to be tougher even than you think."

"Why?"

"I've been having a think about Yalman. I could be wrong, could *easily* be wrong, but I've a feeling he's a phoney."

"For crying out loud! Why?"

"Well, I'm no clairvoyant, but he looked a bit shifty to me. Also, he didn't pay much attention to the discussion we had in Dow-Smith's office. I mean, he didn't seem to care much about the pick up in Nigella. Did you notice?"

Charlie began to pace up and down the room in thought. "Yes, come to think of it, I suppose I did. But remember he wasn't going to be in the pick up party, was he? He wasn't planning to fly out with us."

"No. But if that failed, everything failed. And he just didn't seem interested."

"Sainted aunts, Perry! It's getting worse. Let's find Pinkerton."

They had to wait until well into the morning, after eleven, before they could get a meeting with Pinkerton set up. It took place in Dow-Smith's office again and Pinkerton fluttered about keeping close to the station commander, and going closer still every time Charlie pointed his bristling moustache in the little man's direction. "Gentlemen, it's preposterous, um, with all respect, it's *preposterous* to talk about Refet not being trustworthy. He's highly regarded at the FO —ah, Foreign Office. They've known him for years. I have every confidence." He gave what was evidently intended to be a reassuring smile and Perry, finding his gaze focussed on the cluster of teeth that seemed to push themselves out of Pinkerton's flabby mouth like sailors lining the deck to abandon ship, decided that here was one man who should never smile.

"You've had confidence all along," said Perry. "But we don't like the way he took the kid off alone—don't like it at all. You can assume we now have doubts." When Perry was roused he handled the situation well; there was still the soft, drawly voice, the calmness, the solid confidence of the man, and behind this self control a toughness and determination that came over with a thump. Charlie's word for it was voltage—"Perry," he would say, "you've got voltage there, mate. Voltage!" Perry stood now stooping slightly towards Pinkerton, unnerving the Foreign Office man with the hard expression on his weather-beaten face and the coldness of his grey, unblinking eyes.

Pinkerton waved a hand defensively to and fro, and addressed his next remark to the station commander. "An excess of zeal by Refet, sir. Wrong of him, but well intentioned—no doubt about that. He'll take good care of the lad."

"Perhaps he will," said Perry, throwing a quick cool-it look at Charlie whose neck and face were reddening. "But listen to me carefully." He paused while Pinkerton closed his lips round the clustered teeth. "There's going to be a time limit on this exercise. A short one. And when it runs out I want the whole goddam air force over there to bring him back. Now, tell me *when*."

"Well, it's . . . um . . . difficult to say *precisely*. We expected to get the Demir boy out without delay. Perhaps they're on their way to Nigella now, might even have arrived. Let's give it 'til, um, eleven tomorrow morning."

Perry shook his head slowly. "We'll give it until ten o'clock tonight." He turned towards the station commander. "Then, Air Commodore, it's up to you. We want the boy back, whatever the cost."

Dow-Smith nodded. "I take your point," he said. "I'll have a word with the AOC-in-C this morning. We'll lay something on—something big. Meanwhile, please go on using the officers' mess while you wait."

At seven twenty-two by the mess clock a steward walked up to Perry in the snooker room. "Mr Langhorne?" he asked.

"Yes."

"The Station Commander would like to see you in his office at once please."

"Come on, Charles. Let's go," said Perry, and they hurried across in silence.

Pinkerton was looking more nervous and fluttery than ever and again stood very close to the air commodore. Charlie spoke first. "All right," he said bluntly. "What's the news?"

For once Pinkerton was silent and Dow-Smith nudged him sharply. "Go on," he said. "Tell them."

"Gentlemen, I've . . . um . . . I've had word from London, Sir Hartley himself. And he's heard from Henry Wright in Rabass. I'll not beat about the bush —straight to the point is best." The little man wriggled from an inner agony. "We've been let down. Yes, badly let down. Refet has, um, Yalman has—it's hard, terribly hard to believe—but he's turned against us. Let us down. Badly. Badly. Who *could* have believed it? Years we've known him. Years. I don't know what to say." He looked as if he might cry at any moment.

Charlie stalked across the room towards him, fists clenched. When he spoke he paused between each word, his voice hard and gravelly. "*What-has-happened-to-Jonathan*?" he asked. "*Get-to-the-point.*"

Pinkerton pressed backwards against the wall, Charlie's bulk towering over him. "I regret to say, greatly regret that Jonathan is being held by Yalman, um, with Mahmut. They're hostages, both of them, and still in Kumaree. Poor boys. We'll do everything we can, everything we can. You, Air Commodore, have plans forming already—isn't that, um, right?" The pale lips were trembling and jerking with emotion.

"No. That isn't right. It's an over statement." Dow-Smith was turning the screw in the little man now, too.

"But, but . . . um . . . you've been in touch with the AOC, we're on to London. Every possible, um, stone is being . . ."

Charlie's huge red hands had moved to hold Pinkerton by the front of his jacket and began to rock him slowly forward and back, thumping his shoulder blades against the wall on the backward movement then drawing him close—so close that the spikey moustache touched Pinkerton's face. "You and your creepy friends in London are going to be sorry about this when I've done with you," he said. "You just don't *know* how sorry."

"Leave him alone, Charlie," said Perry. "A punch up with Pinkerton doesn't help. But I know what might. Air Commodore, I want to talk by phone to Peers—to Sir Hartley. Can you put me through right now?"

Dow-Smith pressed a button on his desk and the WRAF officer came in. "Molly, can you put Mr Langhorne through to London? He wants Sir Hartley Peers at the Foreign Office. Track the man down wherever he is."

It took almost an hour for the call to go through, an awkward hour during which the station commander and Perry talked, Charlie paced about the room and Pinkerton sat hunched in a chair as far from the others as he could get. When Peers came through he was as breezy and nerveless as usual, my-dear-chapping and how-are-youing as if nothing mattered more than the social pleasantries of life. But Perry brought the conversation quickly to the point.

"Look, Peers," he said. "I reckon General Cukurova would co-operate if the air force went in on a search job now. He's already lost Ephraim and Mahmut and Jonathan's nothing to him so, as I see it, he's got nothing more to lose by co-operating. You could offer him another million or two in aid to tip the balance. How about it?"

"My dear fellow, you know the saying that great minds think alike? I've never believed it. If there's one sure thing about great minds it's that they *never* think alike. Take Adler and Freud. Even Gilbert and Sullivan—you know they were great minds in their way too—always been very keen on them. By the way, be careful what you say. This telephone line passes through many countries."

"Peers! For crying out loud!" Perry closed his eyes in weary exasperation as he cut in on the ramblings of the Private Secretary to the Secretary of State.

"All right—I'll get to the point." A change came over Sir Hartley's voice now; its soft silveriness remained but was overlaid by a crisper note which Perry remembered from former times and well respected. "I'm thinking the way you are, Langhorne, and I've spoken to the Minister. We're already in touch with the Kumarean government. It seems very likely that we'll have permission to start a search and rescue operation over Kumarean territory very soon—perhaps by midnight. I have to take an incoming call now from MoD, ah, the Ministry of Defence. The wires here are humming. Good night."

Immediately after Perry's talk with Sir Hartley, the AOC came briefly on the scrambler 'phone from the Near East Air Force Command H.Q. in Episkopi for Dow-Smith, and it was obvious that clearance for a search and rescue operation was on its way. Dow-Smith put the receiver down and glanced round at the others. "We're on!" he said. "Molly, get Paddow and Bennet up here fast."

The two men came almost at once and Dow-Smith introduced them. "This is Wing Commander Jimmy Paddow, Commander of Fifty-Six squadron —Lightning mark sixes. And Squadron Leader Pete Bennet of Seventy squadron; his lot fly the big stuff, Hercules and Argosys. Now, let's work it all out. Langhorne, we can put up anything we like, even paratroops and the mountain rescue team. MoD have heard from Henry Wright in Rabass and reckon the kids are somewhere in the Korkar area of Kumaree—here." He pointed to a map on the wall before going on. "Now, look at it. It's a big and rugged area. I can't see any way out of this except a ground search, and that's going to be tough. We can airlift in reconnaissance vehicles, dogs—the lot. But even so, we're in for a slog. Any suggestions?"

"There's something you don't know," answered Perry. "And it might change everything. Jonathan has a SARBE with him and he knows how to use it. If we fly an aircraft in the area he might be able to get the bleeper going. Might. Let's try that first."

Dow-Smith smiled broadly and whunked his right fist into the palm of his left hand in a gesture of delight. "That *is* excellent news. The first lucky break. If we can pinpoint their position from the air we'll move the paras in, and the rest is up to them. I don't think they'll let us down."

But Perry wasn't looking as optimistic as the station commander. "With respect, Air Commodore, that won't do," he said. "I guess there are two main reasons why. First, if we try to shoot this thing out Yalman will cut the kids' throats before we get to them. Second, if we do lift them out in one piece we want to scoot away fast. *Really* fast! I don't see us catching the train."

"All right. So what do you propose?"

"Well, I see the situation like this. Pete Bennet, here, does a routine expanding square search with a SARBE receiver equipped aircraft and the biggest fuel load he can carry. Jimmy Paddow covers with the Lightnings. Later, Charlie and I go in with the Aztec to do the pick up. And that's it. Exit all."

Charlie was looking excited. "Let's get the action started, Perry," he said. "Just let's move."

Dow-Smith had a puzzled expression on his face as his mind worked on Perry's tersely spoken sentences. "Just a minute, Langhorne," he said. "I mean, with everything we've got here, why the Aztec?"

"What else? You're way out of range for the helicopters, but I reckon I'll find somewhere to put Yankee Foxtrot down. And Charlie and I would like to do this our own way. Right Charles?"

"You bet. Just let's go."

Dow-Smith seemed about to argue, then had a change of mind. "I think we're going to have to play a lot of this music by ear," he said. "Peter, which aircraft will you use?"

"The whistling wheelbarrow, sir. The Argosy. She's on thirty minutes' readiness."

Molly put her head round the door. "Near East Operations Controller on the scrambler phone for you, sir." she said.

The conversation was very short, and Dow-Smith spoke only the two words, "understood", and "thanks". "That was clearance from NEOC," he explained. "Immediate. So get going, and good luck."

Paddow and Bennet had a hurried talk on the way out to Argosy Rescue Three-Two, then Bennet climbed aboard the big, twin-boomed aircraft and, one by one, the four propellers began to turn. Perry and Charlie watched from a distance. "Is it going to work, Perry?" asked Charlie. "What are the chances?"

"About one in five."

"Yeah. D'you think Jonno can get that locator beacon going?"

"I just don't know. He'll have a darned good try."

"Now I suppose we've got to hang around again. We always seem to be hanging around waiting for other people. I don't like it. It makes me nervous."

"Yeah. Well, I'm nervous too—if that helps. We won't be hanging around for long. A couple of hours maybe. Then we'll head for Lusquat. Let's find some coffee." They walked back to the officers' mess. Jimmy Paddow joined them for a while. A witty fast talking man, but tough and decisive too; every inch the Wing Commander.

Pete Bennet made himself comfortable in Rescue Three-Two and called the crew on intercom. "You know what this is all about," he said, "so I'll cut the preliminaries. When we reach the search area we will descend to five thousand feet above ground level. Once over the most probable position of the boys, Navigator, I want you to set up the Döppler navigator system to fly an expanding square search with forty mile track spacing. Engineer, you will set up the engines for endurance fuel flow. Co-pilot, select the UHF radio to two-four-three megahertz and we will all listen for the SARBE bleep, a one-second bleep followed by a two point three second pause. The co-pilot will also select ADF for the violet picture presentation—the kicker needle you see here." He pointed towards a dial on each of the pilots' instrument panels. "The needle will kick left if the beacon is to our left and right if it is to our right. When we are in the search area all microphones must be switched off. Clear? Good.

"Now the take-off brief. We will be taking off at ninety-seven thousand pounds with water-methyl injection. Decision speed will be a hundred and nine knots. Before that speed any crew member may call 'Abort' if we have a system malfunction and the take-off will be abandoned. With an engine failure occurring above this speed, the take-off will be continued. Engine de-icing is not required for take-off. We will have Akrotiri AK beacon on both ADF receivers for departure navigation aids. Any questions?"

There were no questions, and so the co-pilot called

the Rescue Coordination Centre. "Cyprus rescue, this is Rescue Three-Two checking in with engines running."

The rescue controller acknowledged. "Roger Three-Two. Get airborne and join airways at Nicosia. Call me again on five-six-nine-five on airways amber two-eight. Your Kumarean Air Force clearance number is Kilo Alpha Foxtrot three-zero-six-four."

More brief radio exchanges took place and then the clamorous Rolls-Royce Darts began to give out some real power and Rescue Three-Two rolled through the darkness towards runway one-one. Shortly before midnight the co-pilot pushed the throttles forward and in a crescendo of noise the heavy aircraft accelerated along the huge strip of concrete, flashing past the runway lights and, at last, lifted off its 97-thousand pounds of weight as delicately as a floating feather and headed towards Kumaree.

North of Nicosia the aircraft made radio contact. "Cyprus Rescue, this is Rescue Three-Two, airborne at twenty-three fifty-seven estimating the search area at zero-two-four-eight. My endurance is seven hours and three-zero minutes."

"Three-Two, roger. Refuel at Lusquat before searching and as required. Facilities have been arranged."

"Cyprus Rescue. This is Three-Two, Wilco."

The Kumarean authorities were co-operative at Lusquat and Rescue Three-Two took off into the search area with full tanks at dawn. The long slog began. North for 40 miles, then east for 40, then south for 80 and west for another 80; then a turn to the north again, and this time, as the square expanded, for 120 wearisome miles; and then east . . . and south . . . and west. And on and on, repeating the cycle over and over. The crew looked down on the random, timeless crags and wondered if there was any hope of finding two boys in terrain like that.

While the search was still in its early stages, Yankee Foxtrot rolled quietly into Lusquat Airport and refuelled. Perry and Charlie were each carrying a heavy Colt forty-five automatic pistol issued to them on the orders of Air Commodore Dow-Smith. There had been some air to air chat on the way with Jimmy Paddow's Lightnings patrolling off the Kumarean coast, but nothing with Bennet's Argosy, Rescue three-two. The weather was turning hot again, with the usual vivid blue sky and just a few slow-moving cumulus clouds casting little shadows on the ground.

Jonathan heard the distant engines for the first time at about eight-fifteen in the morning. It was the third day since he had left the comfortable friendship of Perry and Charlie. Sixty-one hours of hell. Both boys had had pain to endure from their manacled ankles which were swollen and red, and yesterday, during the afternoon, Yalman had hit them several times on the fronts and backs of their legs with a cane. Just a warming up session, Yalman had said, something to be thinking about. Not a touch on the falaka to follow soon if Ephraim didn't come. The night had been passed without as much as a blanket, lying on their backs on the utterly hard rock floor; a primitive oil lamp threw a feeble light on the scene and at erratic intervals Yalman or Eski, who were sleeping somewhere else, would appear in the entrance to make sure that the prisoners were safe. There was no sanitation—just the desolate outdoors. In a way that was the one good thing about the whole wretched situation—the boys were allowed to struggle outside carrying the massive iron balls weighing fifty pounds or more each, the chain tugging painfully at their ankles as it swung about. Outside, for a moment, there was the illusion of freedom.

Yalman and Eski, laughing, Yalman shouting derisive and vulgar advice, had watched them go in the early evening. "Pretend you can't hear them, Jonathan," Mahmut had advised quietly. "They're not worth a thought. Just a couple of thugs." Mahmut had a dignity about him, Jonathan noticed, a dignity that he wore like armour plating. It impressed and helped the younger boy who promised himself he would do as well.

They had talked a good deal during the uncomfortable night as it slowly passed, and come to know each other closely. Mahmut didn't care about aircraft. "Lepidoptera are my hobby," he'd said—and laughed softly. "That's butterflies to you." He told Jonathan enough about butterflies to give him a glimpse of a miniature new world of grace and colour and fragility that helped to take his mind off the pain of the moment and fear of the future.

At about three, after a pause in the conversation, Jonathan suddenly sat upright looking shocked. "Crickey, Mahmut!" he whispered loudly. "I've just remembered something. I'd clean forgotten—in the van I've got a thing called a SARBE beacon and a gun. They're in the zip-up bag. The beacon gives out a bleep—it guides searching aircraft to the spot. And the gun's loaded. A Beretta thirty-eight. Let's get out to the van—*quickly*. Come on!" He was struggling to his feet.

It took Mahmut a moment to tune in. Even then he seemed doubtful. "Be careful, Jon," he said. "I think they may be sleeping in the van. We mustn't make a sound—they'll flay us to pieces if they catch us."

"Come on!" Jonathan had heaved the great ball into the air now and was clutching it to his stomach, staggering towards the exit and roughly cut steps. At the foot of the steps they put the iron balls down and sat for a moment breathing heavily and resting. It was warm out here, away from the chill of the hewn-out rock; a fine clear night with too much moonlight for choice. Jonathan set the pace again as soon as his breath was under control and went lurching off towards the van parked more than a hundred metres away, his bare foot taking heavy punishment on the jagged rocks and stones they were forced to cross.

Near the van, breathless again and with aching backs and an agonising foot and ankle each, they sat down for another rest. A trickle of tears ran down Jonathan's face by now and he was not aware of it.

He did notice that his foot was bleeding a bit and that his breath was coming in strange uncontrollable blasts as if his lungs were reduced to working in spasms. Together they sat, heads on knees, and gulped the gentle night air. It took a minute or two for their chests to stop the hectic heaving, and then they stood up and walked the last few paces to the van and peered into the cab. There was nobody there.

Jonathan put his mouth up to Mahmut's ear and whispered. "We'll go to the back and listen. If we don't hear anyone breathing I'll open the door. Come on." They went round on their hands and knees, rolling and pulling the big iron balls underneath them.

There were no sounds of breathing, and Jonathan reached for the door handle. The pain and excitement had banished fear until now, but it came surging back at this moment of decision and he felt his heart start the pounding and hammering again that seemed to have come so often in the past three days. For a moment he nearly took his hand away again like a swimmer who won't jump in, then, with sudden resolution, opened the door. A black void confronted him, a void that smelled still of animal fat. It was so dark in the van that he couldn't see a thing and he put his head well inside. Yalman and Eski weren't there—that much was certain.

"I'll have to get in," he whispered. "Lift the ball up." Mahmut struggled up with the lump of iron and Jonathan floundered into the blackness. He came back again seconds later. "I've got it," he whispered.

"Look! It's all intact. Lift the ball down." Mahmut lifted it down and then, as Jonathan followed, held out his hand. "Shake," he said. "Bloody well done." They grinned at each other and shook hands. Jonathan felt pleased with himself—and with Mahmut. They were doing all right and at least they had a chance now.

Squatting at the back of the van Jonathan checked the two metal boxes, the yellow one with the batteries and the green and yellow one, the transistorised beacon itself. The beacon had a split pin and ring which he prepared to pull out. "Keep clear," he warned. "The aerial comes out in a rush." Then he pulled, and the spring steel whipped out and uncoiled to stand like a mast about five feet tall.

"Gosh!" said Mahmut. "That certainly moved."

"Yes. It could cut your nose off. It's switched on now, automatically, and we should be bleeping away. I want to get it over there, where Yalman won't see it but it's not too shielded by rocks." Together they crawled beyond the van to a depression in the rocky ground and propped the beacon with stones so that the aerial stood vertical and clear.

As they finished, a rim of light began to show where the sky and earth met. "Look!" said Mahmut. "Dawn's coming up. We'd better get back. Where's the gun?"

"It's still by the van. Let's go."

They paused at the van while Jon tucked the Beretta inside his shirt, threw the zip-up bag back in the van and closed the rear door. Then the slow, pain-

ful struggle back to the obelisk of rock began. Dawn was well under way as they reached the steps and faced the long laborious climb up, puffing, sweating and bleeding. Jonathan went first, lifting the iron ball up two steps at a time, then following himself. Near the top a movement caught his eye and looking up he saw two scuffed shoes and a pair of baggy trousers; looking further up he saw Eski's heavy face. He thanked the good lord it was Eski, who always seemed a bit on the dull side. An easier thug to deal with than Yalman.

"Hullo," said Jonathan innocently, between gulps of air.

"Where 'ave you been?" The man spoke with a heavy accent.

"Just for a walk—you know."

"Don't go too big distance or per'aps misunderstood. Per'aps shot."

Jonathan switched the subject. "We're hungry and thirsty," he said. "And our ankles hurt."

"That is mos' sad, sad. Come inside, stay where always seen. You understood?"

The boys struggled up the last few steps and across the rock floor where they lay on their backs, silent, recovering. Eski ignored them. Half an hour or so later they heard the old van start up and wondered if he was off for another talk with Henry Wright. Eski seemed to do the courier work while Yalman stayed at the rock.

Jonathan had moved the Beretta round to his back, still inside his shirt, where the bulge didn't show; it was most uncomfortable, pressing up against his backbone, but that hardly mattered. Discomfort is relative.

Chapter Eight

WE'LL TRY THAT. PRAY

At eight-fifteen the violet picture kicker needle was kicking hard right in Rescue Three-Two, and Bennet made constant small directional changes to starboard. There was real excitement on board. "I think it must be the kids, all right, skipper," the navigator said. "It's a SARBE signal without any doubt and it's leading us to those high rocks—good cover and all that."

"I'm sure it's them. Certain. Watch the needle. There'll be no signal directly overhead. Locate the position exactly on the chart. Co-pilot, call Lusquat, request Yankee Foxtrot to get airborne. Immediate."

Perry and Charlie ran like colts to Yankee Foxtrot from the met room where they'd been standing when word came through, and four minutes later were airborne. Yankee Foxtrot flew sluggishly with an overload of fuel—a hundred and twenty gallons in the standard tanks and another forty in tins in the back. "She keeps trying to put her tail down," said Perry during the climb.

"Yuh. And she's trimmed nose heavy."

"She'll do it. Just take a little of the back pressure of the stick with me." Charlie put the edge of his hand on the centre of the steering column and pushed gently forward. "Now make a test call," Perry went on. "See if you can pick up Rescue Three-Two on one-two-one decimal five."

"Okay, but it's a long call."

"Yeah. But give it a try."

To the surprise of both of them, Rescue Three-Two came in loud and clear and they recognised the voice of Pete Bennet, who was sounding very calm, very precise.

"Yankee Foxtrot. We have a definite SARBE contact and will lead you to it. We have left the area and are steering three-zero-zero to intercept. Rendezvous over Eban township our estimated nine-zero-five."

Charlie called back. "Roger Rescue Three-Two. Will call you again with our estimate for Eban." Charlie checked his map, got out the circular airman's calculator and worked out the arrival time.

They met as planned over Eban, an exciting moment. Rescue Three-Two waggled its wings in greeting as the Aztec drew near and Perry did the same. The two aircraft then set off together towards Yalman's hide-away, Yankee Foxtrot having to hammer along to keep up with the Argosy in slow cruise. Perry made another transmission. "Rescue Three-Two. Do not overfly the area or we may arouse suspicions. We have visibility twenty/thirty miles in a mountainous area. Request you break away when visual contact is made."

At nine forty-two Rescue Three-Two called again. "The suspected area is now in sight, bearing zero-one-zero from you sixteen miles, obelisk-like rocks. Do you have contact?"

Charlie called back cheerfully. "Rescue Three-Two. Affirmative. We see them. Thank you. Good day."

Bennet took the hint and turned the big aircraft ninety degrees to starboard heading back towards Akrotiri. He sent a farewell message. "Yankee Foxtrot. Good luck. I'll have a drink waiting for you. Listening out on one-two-one decimal five. Out."

It seemed very lonely for a moment as the Argosy's strange and friendly shape dimished into the distance and soon vanished altogether. "I think you're going to have a long walk," Perry said, breaking the conversational silence. "See that?" He pointed ahead three or four miles. "I don't know what that is, but I'm going to have a go at putting her down there."

"It looks pretty weird," said Charlie. "Like a huge dish of salt. Shall we have a gander at it first—low level?"

"No. I don't want to hang around. We're going straight in. Any idea where the wind is?"

"We took off on one-four."

"Yeah. We'll try that, as near as possible. Pray."

"Okay, but put her down nicely. She's got a hell of a load on."

Perry nodded, concentrating now. He throttled back and put gear and flaps down and Yankee Foxtrot began to mush out of the sky. They approached over some wickedly jagged looking rocks and were glad to see them pass safely underneath, then the wheels touched down very gently. A dense cloud of dust billowed out during the ground roll and began to drift over the scene like white smoke. Charlie strained round to look at it. "Good grief!" he said. "I think we're on the moon."

As the aircraft came almost to a stop Perry opened up the starboard Lycoming and trod hard on the left rudder. "She's very sluggish," he yelled. "The wheels must be sinking in." But Yankee Foxtrot struggled round the turn and with throttles half open they taxied back to the downwind end, ready for take-off, and cut the engines.

They clambered out and dropped to the ground. The dust was drifting away towards the edge of the saucer now and thinning out. Charlie glanced round the weird, inhuman landscape. "It doesn't feel like our dear old Lonehead to me," he said. "*No* sir."

Perry was crouching by the starboard wheel. "Look," he said, "she's in, two or three inches. If we want to leave in a hurry that's going to be awkward. If she goes any deeper she might not roll at all."

"Yes. My bet is she'll sink some more. We want to put something under the wheels."

"Right. But what? There isn't anything, is there?"

"What about the petrol cans in the back? We can top the tanks up, then dig them in and roll forward and park on them. She'll take off then I think—if we can start her rolling she'll keep going."

Perry had a special smile for moments like this, a

sudden breaking through onto his weathered face of a humour, natural and infectious, that was always close at hand, lurking beneath the surface of the man and waiting to show. "Charles," he said, "you're a genius and I'm glad I've always said so. Let's get on with it."

It took a full two hours to refuel, dig the cans in and park Yankee Foxtrot on top of them. The morning was well through by the time they finished. Afterwards, they sat for a while resting under the shade of the Aztec's wing. Dow-Smith had given them hip holsters and officers' belts for the Colt forty-fives and now they put them on.

"You scare me, Peregrene," said Charles. "The fastest gun in Bean City. Don't shoot."

"Yeah," agreed Perry. "The last time I fired one of these it was still in the holster, but know what? It blew the guy's toes off."

They set out, walking slowly towards the distant obelisk-shaped rocks. Visibility was good and the distance deceptive. It took a good three hours to arrive nearby. The last half mile was across flat, stone-strewn ground which led up to a curious wall of sepia coloured rock standing about fifty feet high. The ragged surface of the rock made it easy enough to climb, though hot work, and they laboured to the top, then lay observing the scene. There were six obelisks visible, each with a roughly cut entrance leading into what looked like an almost black interior. Nobody seemed to be about. Standing not very far from one obelisk was an old Chevrolet van.

"This isn't the moon as I thought," said Charlie, awed by the sight. "It's Disneyland. Which one d'you think they're in? That one?" He pointed to a rock with a sharply pointed top near the van.

"I'd say so. But let's watch for a while."

"It's hot. An apple would bake up here."

After quite a long wait, a figure appeared from another obelisk near the pointed one.

"That's Yalman," said Perry.

"Yes. I think so."

"I know it. I'd recognise the beggar from five miles. He's paying a visit next door. Look."

"That means the kids are in there, in the pointed one."

"You bet."

"D'you think Yalman's alone?"

"I don't know. He could be. Let's wait a bit longer." For another half hour they lay motionless, the sweat running down the backs of their necks, and watched. Nothing happened. Then Perry decided on action.

"Charlie, this should be pretty straightforward. Look, first we'll go for the van—see what's inside it; I expect there's some hardware in there. Then on up to the pointed rock. We'll wait by the steps. He's bound to come out sooner or later and we've got him. We shouldn't have to fire a shot."

The first part of the attack was difficult, keeping low as they moved round sideways out of the line of sight from the obelisk's entrance. Charlie swore a good deal as he heaved his solid frame along the ragged rock, often right down on his belly. For Peregrene, lean and compact, the effort was less but still quite enough; he'd never been much of a man—or boy—for athletics but he did some now. It was a relief to stand up when, at last, they could risk it. They looked a mess—hair matted down with sweat and clothes torn.

The van lay dead ahead now, pointing towards them. "I think I'll make a sprint for it," said Perry. "Cover me, will you? But take *care* with that forty-five." Charlie hauled the heavy gun out of its holster and pulled the cocking slide back while Perry looked at him doubtfully. "I don't know who scares me more," he said. "You or Yalman. Goodbye," and he was off, loping along towards the van. He got there safely and dropped, panting, into a crouch position, then moved carefully round to the shielded side of the old Chevrolet and climbed into the cab. A few seconds later he was out again, carrying a gun, a big one, and beckoned Charlie over.

Charlie ran, more or less on tip-toe, looking funny but moving fast and quietly. Perry grinned as he flopped to the ground beside him. "You'd have been good at the ballet," he said in a whisper.

"You've found that then." Charlie was looking at the gun.

"Yes. Under the seat. It's a Thompson sub-machine gun. Useful. I knew a man in Bean City who said he'd cut down trees with a tommy gun."

"Yeah, Bean City trees. You can cut them down with a soup spoon."

They walked the hundred feet or so to the obelisk, keeping well to the side, but apart from that as casually as a pair of country ramblers, Peregrene carrying the submachine gun loaded and cocked, Charlie with the forty-five in his hand, safety catch off. Yalman didn't seem to be on watch.

Pressing up against the base of the big obelisk, they moved round close to the steps. The entrance was almost above them now, about eight feet up from the ground. They could hear Yalman swearing—he seemed to be having trouble with a tape recorder. "We'll just wait," whispered Perry. "When he comes out we say 'kindly put your hands up Mr Yalman, sir' and it's all over."

"You could blow one of his ears off first," suggested Charlie.

They had been waiting three or four minutes when a voice from behind said, "Don' turn or shot, very quick shot. Guns down on groun' slow an' gen'ly." A single shot sounded then, very loud and sharp and Charlie jumped with the shock of it. Perry glanced over his shoulder and briefly glimpsed a heavy man standing there with a revolver in his hand, a wisp of smoke was drifting from the barrel. "Do as he says, Charles," said Perry and they bent down to put the guns to the ground.

Yalman appeared then at the top of the steps looking startled, his eyes flickering about taking in the scene. He spoke rapidly in Kumarean and the other man, Eski, spoke back. Yalman calmed down in a moment and leaned against the entrance looking casual. "You could have won then, Langhorne," he said. "We didn't expect callers out here. We must be more careful. Move away from the guns." Perry and Charlie took two or three steps away from the base of the obelisk and had a good look round. Yalman was to the left, Eski to the right, and still holding the revolver—a Smith and Wesson snubnose, Perry decided.

There were points of colour in Charlie's cheeks, the result of shock and anger. "Where are the kids, Yalman?" he asked gruffly. But Yalman answered with another question. "What do you expect me to do with you, Langhorne? I can't keep you prisoner and I can't let you go, so there's only one thing left—isn't there? You're ahead of me I'm sure, but I'll spell it out. You'll have to be shot. We'd better get it over with. Over there I think." He gestured towards the side.

The points of colour disappeared from Charlie's face and he turned very pale. Yalman said something to Eski next in Kumarean, and gave two sideways nods of his head. He was still talking when another shot sounded.

It came from inside the rock and the noise of the explosion cracked out through the entrance with deafening effect. Yalman jerked so hard it looked at first as if he's been hit. Then a boy's hand and Beretta thirty-eight came out of the darkness, and Jonathan was calling louding. "Hi, Perry, Charlie! It's me!" He sounded happy, exultant.

"Good lad!" Perry shouted back. "Stand further

away from him—just a little. Keep out of his reach." Jonathan took one step backwards.

"Well done, Jonno," called Charlie. "Don't take your eyes off him for a second."

Perry looked up at Yalman and smiled. "Well, now," he said. "That's interesting. You're covering us, and we're covering you. Stalemate, eh?"

Yalman never took long to size a situation up and he'd reckoned this one out already. "We'll have to make a deal," he said.

"I guess so." Casually, Peregrene took a step forward, picked up the tommygun then turned towards Eski who seemed stunned by the sudden reverse. "Who's your friend, Yalman?"

"Bin Eski."

"Not your class, I wouldn't have thought. You know, if I squeezed the trigger I could cut him in two right across his belly. We could see what he had for breakfast."

"I don't think so. That's my gun and it isn't loaded."

"Oh yeah? Try me."

Yalman was trying hard to look unconcerned. "Anyway, he'd have time to get a shot in. He's a marksman. One would be enough for you."

Perry laughed. "Well, come on down," he said. "You're giving me neckache. Jonathan, follow him."

"I can't," Jonathan called back, sounding anxious now. "I've got a ball and chain on my foot. Mahmut's here, and he's got one too."

Charlie's face hardened. He picked up the forty-five and strode up the steps, past Yalman who stood hesitating by the entrance. Charlie walked through and crouched down to look at Jonathan's raw and swollen ankle, then went back to the entrance and put the underside of his shoe against the small of Yalman's back, and pushed. Yalman began a frantic stumble, missed his footing and rolled and somersaulted down the hard, uneven steps crashing onto the stony ground near Perry. He hit his face on the way down and lay dazed, bleeding from the nose.

Charlie was standing at the top of the steps pulsing with anger. "You should see these kids, Perry," he called. "That pig has been treating them like galley slaves. They're in chains. Tell him to bring the key up here or I'll pitch him down the stairs again."

"Go on, Yalman," Perry said quietly. "Get it up there."

Yalman lurched to his feet and fumbled for the key. He struggled up a step or two and handed it to Charlie who released the boys.

Perry was shocked, too, when he saw the state of the boys' ankles. "Holy Moses!" he said. "Jonny, you look awful. That must really hurt. Can you walk?"

"Well, a bit. It hurts. But it's great to have that chain off."

"And Mahmut, how are you, mate?"

Mahmut gave a little smile, "Happy, very happy indeed, now that you're here."

Peregrene nodded. "I guess you would be," he said. "Charlie, help them into the van. Mr Yalman and Mr Eski, here, are going to drive us to Yankee Foxtrot. Isn't that right gentlemen?"

Eski was standing with the snubnose Smith and Wesson pointed at Perry, and Perry had the tommy-gun pointing straight back. Yalman, sitting on the ground at the foot of the steps was dabbing away at his face with a bloodstained handkerchief. Both men were silent, so Perry went on. "You've lost, Yalman, and you know it. The deal is this. We keep the guns, all of them, including his"—he gestured towards Eski—"and you drive us to the aircraft. We'll let you go there, and if you know what's good for you, you and your little friend will get as far away in as short a time as that wheezy old van can take you. Clear?" Yalman grunted.

Perry sat in front beside Eski and kept the forty-five in his hand. Charlie held Yalman in the back with the tommygun as a guarantee.

He was still furious, and breathing hard. "I've a good mind to take your leg off with this Yalman," he said, tapping the gun as the van began to clank over the rough ground. "Where shall we cut it, Jonno? Above or below the knee?" Apparently Yalman didn't take in the threat or realised it was an empty one, and there was no reaction.

On orders from Perry, Eski stopped the van a good quarter of a mile away from Yankee Foxtrot and they all got out. "Now, look, Yalman," Perry said. "You two drive off that way." He pointed ninety degrees to the right, away from the Aztec. "And keep going until you're out of sight. Just don't try anything."

Silently Yalman and Eski got back into the van and drove away, not very fast.

"Now listen, everyone. Nobody's to get into the line of sight between me and the aircraft. Is that understood? Keep well over to the left there."

"Why?" asked Jonathan.

"I've a feeling you're going to see why. Walk as fast as you can. Come on."

They covered a few hundred metres and then Perry shouted out. "Look, they're coming back. Out of my way." He flung himself down, grabbing the submachine gun from Charlie as he went. "They're going to ram Yankee Foxtrot. By God, I thought they might." The van had picked up a lot of speed now and was running straight towards the Aztec. Perry pressed the trigger and, with a staccato roar that made your ears hurt and hum, the bullets smashed into the front and side of the straining Chevrolet. The old van went immediately out of control, at first lurching from side to side, swaying precariously, then swinging round an erractic arc that looked for a moment as if it might still lead to a head-on crash into Yankee Foxtrot's rear; but this time the turn continued, the steering seemingly jammed on half lock. With a strangely slow rocking movement, the van went into a roll, going all the way over, and then over and over again, shedding metal and glass with enormous bangs like cannon fire and throwing the limestone dust high into the air. It finished on its back making little sounds, clickings and tickings, like the death throes of a monster beetle. Charlie and the boys stood in silence gaping at the extraordinary sight; it seemed very quiet now, with the firing ended and the van's last, hectic motoring at an end.

Perry spoke first. "I know why they tried that. Yalman really did think the gun might not have been loaded. It had an empty magazine in it when I fished it out from under the seat. But I put a full one in that was on the floor. Yalman sure doesn't like giving up."

"Shall we go over to him?" asked Jonathan.

"There's only one place we're going, Jonno," said Charlie. "And that's into Yankee Foxtrot. We can't get out of here fast enough to suit me."

For Jonathan, with his ankle throbbing and body limp from exhaustion and hunger, it was a moment of rare delight to struggle once more into the friendly back of Yankee Foxtrot, and to see Perry and Charlie start again into the pre flight routines with all their old skill and flair. He fastened his seat belt, helped Mahmut do his, then put on the headset and plugged in. A high temperature had built up in the cockpit and their faces were all quickly wet again with sweat. Nobody minded.

The Lycomings spluttered into life sending a swirling fog of limestone dust out behind. Peregrene warmed the engines for two minutes at fifteen hundred, waggled the control surfaces testing for full and free movement, checked the mags briefly by switching them off and on, one by one, then quickly ran through the pre-flight vital actions, speaking them out as he went. "Throttle friction okay, trim for take-off, mixture rich, cold air, pitch for take-off, fuel on, booster pump on, flap set for take-off, gyros, gauges, hatches all okay. How about harnesses?" He leaned round and put a hand under Jonathan's lap belt, then under Mahmuts. "You can get both those tighter," he said. "Do it. If we hit a soft patch we might end up like them." He gestured towards the shattered Chevrolet already covered in a layer of dust and looking as if it had been lying out there for months.

With the toe brake held firmly down, Perry brought the Lycomings noisily up to take-off revs and Yankee Foxtrot began to shiver and shake, straining to be off, the dust billowing out now like a desert sandstorm. Then he let the brakes go and the aircraft surged forward. As the wheels rolled off the petrol cans and hit the soft limestone it felt as if the brakes were on again, but Yankee Foxtrot kept rolling and the speed slowly built up. At forty knots she was getting a good deal of lift and the wheels were rolling better across the slack surface. Soon after that she lifted off—and touched again, lifted off and touched again and, at last, began a sluggish climb, suffering from the double effect of thin air and a heavy load. Charlie gave Peregrene a friendly knock on the arm and shouted congratulations. "Very pretty. *Very* pretty work! She's away."

They banked left and Jonathan, sitting in the middle row left hand seat, had a last look at the moonscape below, picked out the gaunt obelisk that had been their prison, saw again the wreckage of the Chevrolet, and a shudder rippled up his backbone.

Yankee Foxtrot levelled out and the scene of desolation vanished. The worst three days of his life were dropping away beneath them. He thanked heaven for all the good things ahead—like a hot bath, for example, and a solid meal—bangers and mash for choice—and a very long sleep. He glanced towards Mahmut. "Are you all right?" he asked.

"Yes, thank you. Fine." Mahmut look very composed.

"My ankle still hurts. Does yours?"

"Yes."

"Well, I expect they'll do something for us at Akrotiri." They lapsed into a tired silence.

With the altimeter showing an unreliable six thousand feet, Perry steered two-three-zero, magnetic. The coastline was in sight ahead, and Charlie reckoned they had three hundred and twenty nautical miles to go. Dusk began to shade the sky and, after a brief discussion, Perry and Charlie decided to switch on the navigation lights. "See if you can call Lusquat," said Perry. "Tell them about Yalman and his buddy."

"Not a hope from here."

"Just try it."

But Charlie proved to have been right. After four calls there was no response from Lusquat control. "It looks as if we're on our own," he said.

"Not quite," replied Perry. "What are those?" He pointed forward right and everyone looked. Three sets of wingtip lights were approaching from the direction of central Kumaree and closing very fast.

Charlie was first to make a positive identification in the half dark sky. "MiGs," he said. "MiG twenty-ones. What in heck's up with them?"

One MiG stood off, circling, while the other two swept round behind the Aztec. They had trouble getting their speed back to match Yankee Foxtrot's stately cruise of 155 knots and had to break away the first time and try again. Then the leader came alongside on the left, gear and flaps down, nose high in the air and engine smoking. He'd got his speed cut to one-five-five. The second MiG was lurking behind, like a sheepdog.

"We've got problems," said Perry. "They're Kumarean airforce and they're giving us an invitation to join them for dinner. A goddam pressing invitation I would think. Our friend on the left here will flash his lights, rock his wings and break away at right angles in a minute, then come back. That's the international drill. Watch him."

"What's it all about?" asked Charlie.

"Just an old fashioned double-cross, I'd say. Our friend Cukurova wants Mahmut back. We're to have the honour of delivering him."

At that moment the MiG went into sudden left bank and steered away on about one-four-zero. He held a short leg of two miles or so, then came curving back into formation with Yankee Foxtrot again.

Mahmut and Jonathan had turned very pale. Charlie looked grim and angry, clenching and unclenching his large hands. Perry showed almost nothing of his feelings but he was sitting very alert and straight in his seat. "That was the invitation," he said.

"What are you going to do?" asked Charlie.

"Just keep going for the moment, and pretend we don't understand. I'll give him a friendly waggle." He put on heavy amounts of aileron, left right, then left right again, and Yankee Foxtrot waved what looked like a cordial greeting.

For a short time nothing happened. "I don't like this," said Charlie. "Shall I send out a Mayday call?"

Before Perry answered twin streams of tracer cannon flashed from the formating MiG drawing strangely beautiful lines of light stretching ahead and fading gradually into nothing. Perry made up his mind. "Yes," he said. "Call Mayday. Quick."

Charlie had already selected the international distress frequency, one-two-one decimal five, and now he pressed the transmit button and made the call. "Mayday. Mayday. Mayday. This is Aztec Golf Alpha Romeo Yankee Foxtrot transmitting on one-two-one decimal five. We are being attacked by Kumarean fighters. We have crossed the Kumarean coast south west of Eban. Height six thousand. Heading two-three-zero at one hundred and fifty-five knots. Mayday. Mayday. Mayday."

The MiG on Yankee Foxtrot's left had dropped back a little and now fired a series of cannon bursts that whistled past the wingtip dangerously close.

"That's twenty-three millimetre stuff," said Perry. "The swine's going to shoot us down."

Mahmut leaned forward, still very pale and looking nervous, but under control. "You'd better go with them," he said. "There's no point in everyone getting killed for me."

Perry ignored him and switched off the navigation lights. "Now listen everybody," he said. "I'm going to corkscrew. The Lancasters used to do it in the war. It's quite rough so keep your belts tight. Here we go."

He pushed the control wheel hard forward and turned it left putting on heavy aileron and then, as Yankee Foxtrot went into a sixty degree bank, came in with a bootful of left rudder. The aircraft fell away into a diving turn left and the negative G seemed to Jonathan to send his stomach up to his mouth—he lifted irresistibly out of his seat, straining against the lap belt. Five hundred feet wound off the altimeter in barely six seconds and a stream of tracer cannon from the MiG missed by a mile forming white lines in the sky away to the right and high. Then Perry slapped on opposite aileron and rudder and, moments later, pulled back strongly on the wheel.

The dive was checked now with rivet-popping violence, and Jonathan felt the pressures reverse. His belly ceased pushing against the lap belt, his bottom went heavily downwards into the seat, his chin sank onto his chest, his arms grew leaden and his eyes dimmed. Yankee Foxtrot must have been pulling three and a half G as she struggled out of the dive into a climbing turn right, and her wings bent upwards by inches, perhaps as much as a foot at the tips. Charlie turned to Peregrene. "Jeeze!" he said.

They went over the top of the climb like the biggest big dipper ever imagined and started away again into a diving turn left. Jonathan seemed to feel his stomach depart a second time on its journey up his throat to his mouth, and there was more uncomfortable straining against the lap belt. "Oh lord," he said to himself. "Don't let it happen. Don't let me be sick." He'd forgotten about his ankle.

Unexpectedly the MiG leader broke radio silence and came through on one-two-one decimal five. His accent wasn't easy to read. "Yankee Foxtrot I 'ave air-to-air mizziles. My order eez zwitch on nav lidez theeze momend. Zteer tree-two-sero-for Luzquat. We will accompy. I 'ave you in good zight. Izz understood."

Perry was pulling Yankee Foxtrot over the top of the third corkscrew movement when the call came in. "I guess we're beaten," he said. "They hold the aces."

But another call came through just afterwards, and it was loud and clear enough for them to recognise Jimmy Paddow's voice. "Tally ho, Yankee Foxtrot. Romeo Quebec Charlie Zero-Seven and one playmate approaching you at mach one-point-four. I have you on radar. Keep flying. Estimate you in two minutes. We'll take those MiGs out."

Yankee Foxtrot fell out of the sky again, the glowing instrument needles swinging wildly round the dials. The port wing and the nose went down, the rudder took some more of Perry's boot and the altitude needle began its quick unwind. Charlie pressed the transmit button. "Glad to hear you Zero-Seven. Make their eyes water for us mate." Then there was more pressure, and the deflecting of the wings, and Yankee Foxtrot was hauling out of the dive and starting the full throttle climb. Jonathan found himself swallowing a lot of air and couldn't stop.

The two 56 Squadron Lightnings came from underneath the MiGs at immense speed, flashing up past the Kumarean's noses, their navigation lights burning brightly and leaving red and green streaks behind them that seemed to have more to do with rocketry than aircraft.

Perry stopped the corkscrew pattern, switched on his own lights and trimmed Yankee Foxtrot straight and level at an indicated four thousand two hundred feet and maximum cruise speed. Glancing round, he saw the MiGs. They were too close for comfort, at about the same height and quarter of a mile or so to the right. Very quickly the Kumarean leader banked left, passed under the Aztec and appeared again at Perry's port wingtip back in the menacing formation as before.

Paddow, a good four thousand feet higher, circled left and came arcing round and down to take up station on the left of the MiG. It was a beautiful manoeuvre, shedding speed all the way, pushing out full flap, trimming nose up and bringing the turbo jet revs steadily back to slow idle on one engine and fast idle on the other. Perry could see the massive outline of the Lightning clearly against the dark backdrop of the sky, its nose grotesquely high, hanging on to controllable flight by a mere 10 or 20 knots at 180. Playmate Two had circled right and was stationed now to the rear, tailing, with the second MiG for company. Both Lightning pilots had had to bring in full power again—carefully, carefully, for fear of a flame-out—to remain in flight at all.

A huge grin had spread across Charlie's face, and he shook his head delightedly. "What a bee-utiful sight," he said. "Bee-utiful! God bless the RAF. I don't know where they came from but I'm glad, glad, glad they're here."

Perry was smiling too, quite a relaxed smile—as if he'd just enjoyed a little after-dinner joke at the flying club ball. "They were a jump ahead of us, Charlie. That's the truth of it. They know the general's little ways and hung around. They must have had problems doing it, too—you can't keep these overgrown fireworks in the air for long."

"They must have run a shuttle."

"Yeah. Anyway, we weren't very smart."

"We can't win every time, and we're doing all right mate. What happens next?"

"I dunno. Those MiGs are getting a long, long way from home."

"Yes—you're right. That could get interesting."

Suddenly the lead MiG fired off another burst of tracer cannon, and the white lines were reaching far ahead again and fading, with the same deceptive beauty.

"Now, now," said Charlie mockingly. "Don't be edgy."

WE'LL TRY THAT. PRAY

Paddow smiled and reached for the hexagonal weapon selector switch beside his right knee, and turned it to "guns". He moved the safety switch on the control stick to "off", hooked his index finger round the curved trigger on the front of the stick—and squeezed. With a roar like a thunderclap at your elbow twin cannon began a massive shoot-up—eleven hundred rounds a minute of high explosive shells; ten seconds of that would split a house down the middle. Then Playmate Two joined in, and the sky seemed full of shells.

Perry kept his eyes focussed unfalteringly on the MiG's wingtip positioned just seven or eight feet from his own. He noticed it at once when the MiG began a slow, very slow but quite definite turn to the right across his path and heading him off. Involuntarily, he put on a touch of left aileron and Yankee Foxtrot began a shallow turn in unison. "No you don't, you clever swine," muttered Perry. "I'm not going, thanks. Not tonight," and he pushed the control wheel roughly forward. Down went Yankee Foxtrot's nose again and then, with heavy use of aileron, he banked left, slid under the MiG and Lightning and pulled up again on the other side of Paddow.

Paddow found himself flying now between Perry and the MiG. He nodded and grinned approvingly at the smoothness of the switch. "Neat, neat," he said out loud, talking into his microphone but not transmitting. "Good stuff, Yankee Foxtrot."

The second Lightning saw an instant opportunity and began to change position also, diving and banking left and sliding underneath in a repetition of Yankee Foxtrot's move. It was becoming an aerial ballet this, most carefully rehearsed one would have thought from its precision and grace and sense of form. Playmate Two hauled quickly up and took station a little astern of Yankee Foxtrot, about twenty feet lower and tucked in closely on the left. The Aztec was nicely boxed now, with a protective Lightning on either side. Peregrene, Charlie and the boys laughed at the quick outwitting of the Kumareans. And nobody had been hurt.

The leading MiG put on speed, climbed steeply then orbited overhead for perhaps two minutes, the others standing off, keeping their speed right down and looking awkward and nonplussed. At last they turned together through a slow half circle and headed back to Lusquat and whatever reception their frustrated general and leader might have waiting for them. "Goodbye friends," said Charlie on the intercom as their navigation lights disappeared. "Don't be too late home."

Soon after the MiGs flew off, Paddow waggled his wings and Charlie, on a hunch, turned up the sound on one-two-one decimal one and picked up Paddow making repeat test calls. "Yankee Foxtrot Yankee Foxtrot. Romeo Quebec Charlie Zero-Seven. Are you reading?"

Charlie pressed the button and almost shouted back in his excitement. "Zero-seven. Yankee Foxtrot. Reading you five. Thanks, Jimmy. A great piece of work."

"Yankee Foxtrot. Zero-Seven. Our pleasure. What passengers do you have on board? What is their condition?

"Zero-Seven. Yankee Foxtrot. We are four. Captain Langhorne and co-pilot Thompson, Jonathan Kane and Mahmut Demir. Everybody fit."

"Yankee Foxtrot. Zero-Seven. All copied. We have a fuel problem now and must resume normal cruising. We usually taxi at this speed. Will report your position and ETA to Akrotiri. Good evening." The heavy Lightnings accelerated away into the night sky and Yankee Foxtrot was alone again.

"Those guys impress me, Charles," said Perry. "They've got a good fifteen hundred miles an hour in those blowtubes and they throw them about like doughnuts."

"Yeah, that's right. And the stuff they carry. You're supposed to be a professor just to handle the weapons systems."

"Wouldn't do for you then, eh, Charlie?"

Charlie ignored the joke and they flew on towards Akrotiri in velvety air, their minds contentedly dwelling again on the hot baths, drink, food and softly sprung beds awaiting them at the base. Jonathan and Mahmut were very tired and dozed off despite the pain that still came from their swollen ankles. The big Lycomings were running well, set for fast cruise on a manifold pressure of twenty-three inches and twenty-three hundred revs—about a hundred and seventy knots.

At thirty-two minutes past midnight, Perry made a

sudden change of course, right, and pointed ahead. "That's Cyprus coming up," he said. "See the lights?"

Charlie peered forward and nodded. "That's a very good sight. Let's just keep her rolling."

"I reckon we've about a hundred and twenty to go. How are the kids looking?"

Charlie glanced round at them. "Asleep," he said. "How about you? D'you want to put your head down for a while?"

"Thanks—I'm a bit bushed. Are you okay?"

"Yes, good enough. I've got her."

Gratefully, Peregrene let go the controls and closed his eyes for a catnap.

In about half an hour they were edging into VHF range of Akrotiri tower and began picking up faint radio messages—routine calls to service aircraft arriving and departing. It wouldn't be long now, and Charlie could see the steam from the officers' quarters bathroom billowing round in the back of his mind. Then, abruptly, one of the calls had Perry sitting up very straight. "That's for us," he said.

"Yeah. Deal with it—will you?"

Perry pressed the transmit button. "Akrotiri. Yankee Foxtrot. Reading you three."

The controller came back speaking slowly and precisely to help reception. "Yankee Foxtrot. You are urgently requested to divert to pick up your passenger from Nigella. Can you comply and what is your endurance?"

Perry pressed the button again. "Akrotiri. Stand by."

Charlie was sitting as rigid as if he'd just had an electric shock in the back of his neck. "For crying out loud, Perry!" he said. "They want us to go straight on to Nigella to do that dicey pick-up now? Just like that? It's flipping well not on. I want some kip, that's what."

"I know how you feel."

"Well, we're flipping well not going. Not *now*. To-morrow night perhaps but not now. I'll tell them."

"Just a minute. There must be a new problem, I guess," went on Perry. "Something must have gone badly wrong for them to do this to us now. Charlie—we've got the fuel."

"Blimey! We're going. Aren't we?"

Perry put Yankee Foxtrot into a steepish turn left, about rate two, and transmitted again. "Yankee Fox-trot. I have four hours and am setting course for Nigella turning to zero-six-zero. EET one hour and say forty minutes. Request Nicosia QNH." He settled himself as comfortably as he could in the seat and throttled back to economical cruise at twenty-two inches and twenty-two hundred revs.

"Yankee Foxtrot. Understood. QNH is one-zero-one-two. Please keep radio silence but call in emerg-encies. Out." So that was that. The world seemed to have gone again.

Jonathan, dozing with his headset on, had heard it all. He leaned forward and tapped Charlie on the shoulder. "Swop places with me, Charlie," he said. "You and Perry must be dog tired. I'll fly for a while." He looked questioningly at Perry. "Is that okay?"

"Sure. Great."

Charlie's efforts to shift his large bulk over the seat-backs might have been funny if they hadn't all been so exhausted but he made it after a two or three minute struggle, and Jonathan settled in the front, pushing the inflatable cushions into place and reaching contentedly for the wheel and rudder bar. "I have control," he said calmly.

"Okay, Jon. Hold her on zero-six-two at six thousand, a hundred and fifty-five knots." He turned the nav lights to "off".

Jonathan fixed his eyes on the green-glowing instruments, holding them firm and steady after a half minute or so of hunting about as he settled down. The night air, free of thermals and other turbulence, was marvellously smooth so there was no excuse for rough flying. He concentrated hard on getting everything right. Probably Perry and Charlie wouldn't say much about it—but they would notice everything, every change of speed, or height or heading. They cruised on through the starlit sky in silence except for the steady thrum of the cruising Lycomings. A half moon was up now, throwing a cold glitter on Yankee Foxtrot's wings.

Peregrene studied a map intensely for some time with the help of a cockpit light, then settled down for another half-wakeful, half sleeping catnap. After fifty-five minutes he sat up, leaned over and patted Jonathan's knee. "Okay, Jonny boy," he said. "That was good. I have control now." And Jonathan let go.

It was a relief to sit back again idly, but the pain in his ankle seemed worse. He turned round for a word with Mahmut then gave that thought up; the older boy was asleep.

They crossed the coast and you could see it clearly, a thin line of phosphorescent foam tracing the interface of land and Mediterranean.

Charlie leaned forward. "Nigella," he said. Perry nodded and tuned in the Mubuk VOR Beacon, then gave Jon a ten degree change of course to starboard, and Charlie spoke again. "How long, Perry?"

"Oh, fifty minutes. Maybe forty-eight."

"Shall I come forward and do a bit of driving?"

"I wouldn't bother. Mr Kane can put the gear down for me." Jonathan was pleased about that and had a quick look at the wheel shaped gear control lever beside his left knee at the side of the throttles consul.

"How's the fuel?" asked Charlie. There was a trace of concern in his voice.

"A bit tight."

"You can say that again, mate." The silence returned, and Perry switched on the map-reading light from time to time, studying the charts. He was working hard, several moves ahead in the dangerous game they were about to play—although his face, weathered and somehow leaner looking than ever in the narrow pool of reflected light, showed no visible signs of fatigue or worry. Jonathan pondered for a while about nerves. Difficult to know what another man felt, only how he looked. Certainly it helped to have Perry looking like that. He might have been on the Hammerton run with engine spares on a summer's afternoon and Roz keeping the coffee warm, for all you could read in his face. They flew on, far inland.

"We're close," Perry said at last. "Look out for a little lake—it should show up pretty well tonight. It's sort of kidney-shaped. Know what a kidney looks like, Jon?"

"Yes. Like a bean."

"Well, keep looking."

Mahmut woke up and the four of them scanned the night scene beneath them. Jonathan's sharp eyes spotted the lake first, ahead and to the right, maybe seven or eight miles away.

"That's fine," said Perry. "Now listen. I don't want to scare anyone but this isn't going to be easy. We've got to land on the top of a three thousand foot high mountain near the lake. Table Mountain we used to call it. It's been cut off by weather or something across the top and it's fairly flat. There are a couple of snags though. First, we've got to come in over much higher mountains still and that makes a sweat of the approach; second, we've got nothing to spare on the ground roll—nothing at all. If we overshoot, we fall off the end into the valley, and that's a very quick journey straight down—if you get my point. Now, I'm going to make one trial pass and then we're going in. On the approach I want no conversation, *none*, unless you see something really bad, like a wing coming off. Jonathan, when I say full flap, I want *full* flap and I want it *at once*. We need the sink rate of a barn door. Clear?"

"Yes, Perry." Jonathan put his left hand experimentally on the short flap lever on the other side of the throttle consul, by Peregrene's knee.

"And Jonathan, turn the instrument lights to minimum. It's going to be dark in here."

"Yes, Perry."

"Right, let's have a look round." Perry put Yankee Foxtrot into a shallow dive towards a ragged range of mountains dead ahead. At an indicated six thousand two hundred feet they cleared one peak so narrowly that Jonathan reckoned they might clip the tips of some ghostly shapes on its top—probably trees. A mile or so further on and far below was Table Mountain. It sat in the middle of a ring of other mountains like the inner keep of a castle surrounded by defensive walls. They were shedding height at a thousand feet a minute and Perry went into a steep turn left over the landing area, peering over the wingtop at the dimly discernible scenery below. "I've got the picture again," he said. "Let's get it over with." They climbed away, clearing the peaks on the other side of the basin comfortably, then circled left to fly a normal circuit pattern reducing speed to 105 knots. Jonathan felt a tingle of apprehension, but nothing too serious, and it took his mind off his ankle, which didn't seem to be improving.

"How are we for wind?" Charlie was leaning forward looking grave but calm as he put the question.

"Funny thing about that," replied Perry. "It always seems to be about zero-six which suits us nicely. I guess it funnels through the peaks somehow. But cross your fingers if you like. Okay, Jonathan, let's have the gear down."

Jonathan grabbed the undercarriage lever and pushed it down. A yellow indicator light went out and then, seconds later, three greens lit up. "Gear down and locked," he said briskly.

Perry ran on through the checks and when he called for half flap Jonathan was ready and reached over to set it, watching the indicator needle swing round the flap dial in front of him as the lever went down. Responding to the changed configuration of the wings, Yankee Foxtrot began to push her nose up and Perry wound the trim handle in the roof to keep her level and take back pressure off the stick. Moments later they were steeply banked and turning cross wind, then turning again for the start of the final approach. They all sat very tense and silent as Yankee Foxtrot plodded towards the high peak they had to clear before descending. A sickening vision came into Jonathan's active mind of his own head being smashed against the glowing panel before him, and the prickles of apprehension sharpened; then he forced himself to think about the flaps. He'd kept his hand on the lever, ready to bang them on full the moment Perry spoke.

As the peak came near, Perry switched on the landing light and there it was, with its scrubby top, suddenly lit up and flashing by a dozen or so feet beneath the wheels and, after that, the black void of the valley on the other side. "Full flap!" called Perry and hauled the throttles closed. Jonathan rammed the lever down and held it there; with the speed back to a hazardously low sixty-five knots, Yankee Foxtrot began to sink out of the sky, the stall warning light flashing and the whole aircraft quivering from the diminished airflow across the wings. "Keep the throttles closed for me," said Perry. "Right back on the stops." And Jonathan took one in each hand and held it back.

Perry sat as cool as ever, both hands on the wheel, sensing the aircraft and almost being part of it, picking up a wing with a dab of rudder almost before it had begun to drop and steering with perfect precision for a spot he couldn't see, just left of centre on the nearer edge of Table Mountain, the spot where Yankee Foxtrot *had* to put her wheels on the ground.

Soon the landing light was picking out the flatness of the mountain top and they were close to the critical moment of touch-down. Perry flicked Jonathan's hands away and took the throttles into his own. Very near the end he put on a burst of power to check the rate of descent and there, suddenly, stood the mountain, floodlit and menacing, a huge wall of rock that stretched down into the contrasting darkness of the valley and which seemed to rush towards them at collision height; and then they were over it, floating across the edge like thistledown, and Yankee Foxtrot's nose was coming smoothly up flaring out for a landing and, at last, there it was, the utterly thrilling sound of the wheels in contact. Yankee Foxtrot raced across the rough rock top, banging and shaking and slowing down as Perry pressed away as hard as he dared at the toe brakes. They stopped two hundred feet or so from the far cliff edge and paused, the big fans idling quietly.

Jonathan let out a long, deep, noisy breath of relief as the almost unbearable tension of the last few minutes faded. Charlie leaned over and patted Perry on the arm. "The Lonehead ace does it again, mate! I'd call that an okay landing. A flippin' well okay landing." Mahmut, less aware than the others of the risks of the approach, smiled and gave little approving nods of his head. They were down. A landing you could walk away from. A very good landing indeed.

Perry brought the starboard throttle forward and put on full left rudder. With a roar of controlled power, Yankee Foxtrot turned and rolled back to the touch-down point and headed up into wind again, ready for take off. He switched everything off and then, sitting in the darkness and sudden silence, wiped his face with the palms of his hands.

It was the only sign he gave of what he'd just gone through.

Chapter Nine

COMPANY

Over to the right of Table Mountain a light flashed twice, then twice again.

"Look, Perry," said Charlie softly. "We've got company."

"I guess we have. I wonder who."

"Demir, d'you suppose?"

Mahmut leaned forward. "You think that's my father?" he asked, a big smile spreading across his face.

"I don't know," said Perry. "Let's go see. Jonathan, let me out. Charlie, take the front seat, will you? We may have to fly out of here fast. Start the engines up again." He strapped the big pistol round his waist. "I don't like these goddam guns," he said plaintively.

Jonathan scrambled out onto the wing and jumped to the ground. "I'm coming with you," he said as Perry followed him down.

"No, Jon. You'd better . . ."

"*Yes*, Perry." Jonathan stood there, looking very small in the dim light against Yankee Foxtrot but also determined and calm. "You *need* two people," he went on. "Charlie must stay where he is so I've got to come."

Perry shook the boy's head, and rumpled his hair, gently, appreciatively. "All right then. But keep close to me. Come on, let's go for a walk."

"Just a minute." Jonathan climbed back onto the wing and poked his head through the door, re-appearing in a moment with the other Colt forty-five. "Oh, my God!" said Perry. "That'll knock you over if you use it."

"No it won't."

"Well, don't point it near me."

They walked off into the darkness, across Table Mountain towards the spot where the light had flashed, Jonathan limping slightly, but otherwise both looking nonchalant and unhurried like a couple of tourists out for a stroll. After they had covered about a hundred metres Peregrene grabbed Jonathan's forearm and they both stopped. "Did you hear that?" he asked.

"Yes. An engine or something." The shiver ran up Jonathan's spine again and the hair on the back of his head bristled. They stood, like statues, listening.

"There's something going on in the valley," said Perry. "Let's just lie down a minute and watch. Go on, down on your stomach." They both dropped flat against the stony ground and lay silently. Certainly there was an engine—were several engines perhaps—somewhere down in the darkness of the valley. Then the light flashed again, twice, and was apparently moving slowly towards them. Perry hauled the forty-five out of its holster and pulled back the slide to load a shell into the breech. Jonathan did the same, and felt his heart already pounding and that unpleasant touch of dryness coming back to his mouth. "What do we do next?" he whispered.

"I don't know," Perry whispered back.

They lay without moving for a minute or two more. Then a curious muted call came from the right, a voice they could just hear over the distant idling of Yankee Foxtrot's Lycomings. "Hullo there!" it shouted. "Is anyone there? This is Henry Wright. Is anyone there?"

Perry rose quickly to his feet. "Hullo," he called softly back. "We're over to your right." The light flashed again and Perry and Jonathan headed briskly towards it.

There was something quaint, almost amusing about the encounter in the darkness of the two parties who had never met before—a replay of the famous "Dr Livingstone I presume" situation of Stanley at Ujiji, but nobody laughed. Henry introduced himself in the quiet, to-the-point manner he always showed, and then did the same for Ephraim Demir who shook hands with Peregrene. "What news is there of my son?" Demir asked in a voice sounding strained and tired. "You see I can't leave here until I know he is safe."

Perry gestured towards Yankee Foxtrot. "He's right over there," he said. "Waiting for you in the aircraft." Demir seemed not quite to be taking the words in, as if he feared his senses were tricking him, so Perry reassured him again. "Mahmut's okay. We've got him with us."

Demir wiped a hand across his face. "What marvellous news," he said. "Marvellous! I do thank you for what you've done."

"Who's that?" Perry was peering at the stooped figure of Ismet standing in the background.

"That's my servant, Ismet," explained Demir. "He's in danger here and I would like to take him with us."

"Right. Fine. We can manage that." Perry walked over and shook hands with the old man, who beamed with embarrassed pleasure. In more than seventy years of life, Ismet had never shaken hands with an effendi before.

Henry Wright spoke again, and there was a quiet urgency to his voice. "Look, you'd better get moving quickly," he said. "The army's on to us. That's a patrol you can hear, out looking for Demir. They'll have seen your landing—bound to have done." The engines were much closer now and occasional shouts could be heard.

"Can they get up here?" asked Perry.

"Yes, with a struggle. They'll have to come up the last bit by foot."

An agonising thought gripped Peregrene's mind. To take Henry with them would overload Yankee Foxtrot and seriously reduce the chance of a successful take-off; to leave him behind might mean his death. Six lives against one. And yet there was really no choice. "Mr Wright," he said, "you're coming with us. Come on everyone, into the aircraft."

But Henry stood still, shaking his head and wearing his sad little smile. "I know how to look after myself," he said. "And my whole life is here. Thanks for the offer but I'm not going with you. Now hurry up. For heaven's sake, get away." He took a gun from inside his shirt, cocked it, turned and walked back, retracing the path he and his party had taken.

Perry knew the decision was firm, that argument wouldn't change it. "Good luck—Henry," he called. "Take care man."

Then he turned to the others. "Run for it," he said. "Get a move on." They started to jog trot towards Yankee Foxtrot, and soon discovered that Ismet couldn't wind up to more than a two or three mile an hour hobble. Perry called out to Jonathan to run ahead with Demir. "We'll follow," he added. "Go on, quick!" The boy, whose strong legs and slender shape gave him a high top speed when he wanted it, adjusted to the middle-aged politician's canter, and together they closed on Charlie and the Aztec.

"Take my arm," said Perry to the old man, who clutched it and managed a minor increase of speed.

"I'm grateful, effendi," gasped Ismet.

"Just do your best. We've got time."

But time was what they didn't have. As they neared Yankee Foxtrot a dozen or more lights appeared, swaying about near the right hand rim of the mountain, where Henry would have been. The thrum of the big Lycomings blotted out the sounds but it was obvious there was plenty going on.

Perry and Ismet lurched up to the starboard wing to find Charlie hanging out of the door. "Give the old boy a shove up from behind," he yelled. But Ismet couldn't find the suppleness to lift his foot onto the wing, and began to shield his face from the slipstream which seemed to bother him.

"For God's sake *shove*!" roared Charlie again in exasperation. Then, coming out onto the wing, he put his ham-like hands under the old man's arms and hauled him bodily up and bundled him through the door. Jonathan was waiting in the middle pair of seats and took over the job, pulling the by now very confused Ismet fully in and getting him settled.

Nimbly and speedily—despite his heavy frame—Charlie dropped into the front left seat, checked that the brakes were firmly on and began to move the throttle levers forward. Perry found himself almost blown in by the gale of wind from the starboard propeller, and the door slammed shut. "Let's go, boy!" he shouted, and the Lycomings wound up to their full, thunderous power.

Charlie released the brakes and, as Yankee Foxtrot bounded forward, snapped on the landing light. Suddenly Table Mountain was floodlit and there were soldiers everywhere. It didn't seem real; like a military pageant. Then Jonathan called out. "Look—there's Mr Wright!" And indeed there he was. As they gathered speed, thumping and shaking over the rough face of the rock, Jonathan could see Henry in the centre of a ring of torches, his hands in the air. Then he saw new blobs of light, little flashes of flame, and Henry fell. In a moment the torches were pointing downwards at something on the ground. It took a moment for the truth to break through, and then Jonathan moaned and covered his eyes. "Oh no, no," he said. "They've shot him. They've shot Mr Wright."

The probing headlight showed that the rim of Table Mountain was very close and Charlie was coming in with back pressure now, willing Yankee Foxtrot into the air. She made it with perhaps a hundred feet to go, and roared over the blackness of the valley climbing well. "Nicely done, Charles," said Perry blandly, turning the headlight off. "Steer two-two-five for Akrotiri."

Mahmut called something from the back seat and Perry twisted round. Two bullets had slapped through the after part of the fuselage from the right, missing Mahmut and his father by barely three feet. Perry looked surprised at first, then nodded philosophically and was turning back to the panel when he saw Jonathan's distress. "What is it, Jonny boy?" he asked, and Charlie glanced quickly round too.

"They shot Mr Wright."

"They did? I didn't see it." After a pause he rumpled the boy's bedraggled looking hair. "The world's full of savages, Jonathan," he said. "Have a good cry about it if it helps." He turned back to the panel and in a minute or two Jonathan had himself under control and was sitting up straight watching the dawn come back to the sky.

When they called "finals" at Akrotiri they had almost no useable fuel left—two gallons at the most in Perry's opinion. But Charlie made another greaser of a landing on two-nine, and they turned off and parked at Bravo Dispersal without fuss, like the end of a routine freight flight from Lonehead.

Dow-Smith drew up in a staff car alongside as the heavy steel propellers stopped. He shook hands with Peregrene, Charlie and Jonathan very warmly as, one by one, they hopped out, and then murmured a welcome to the Demirs and old Ismet. "We have a little reception waiting for you in my office," the station commander said. "Are you all right for five minutes before you get away to bed?"

"The kids need medical attention," said Charlie. "Have a look at their ankles."

But Jonathan didn't want to spoil it. "We're all right for a few more minutes," he said, and Mahmut gestured agreement.

"Good. Let's all pile into the car."

As they filed through the office door, a figure rushed at them. They were amazed to see it was Roz, looking very pretty and tearful. She kissed Perry and Charlie, then hugged Jonathan and went on hugging him, standing there laughing and crying and shaking her head. It was a good moment to see her, a very powerful moment for them all. And there was somebody else in the room. Waiting unobtrusively in the corner was Sir Hartley Peers himself. Perry boggled, then walked across to him. "Well, I'll be darned," he said. "If it isn't Mister Bigsville in person." They shook hands firmly and with genuine warmth.

When they'd all calmed down, Sir Hartley made what amounted to a little speech. He thanked them, congratulated them and then, with his big bland smile, reminded them of the Official Secrets Act which still applied. "So I'm afraid you can't say much about it all," he said. "There'll be a formal statement from the Ministry and that must be the end of that. Ah yes, except for one thing." The beam was bigger and sunnier than ever now. "The three of you are all to receive a decoration. I'm not at liberty to tell you what it is, but you, Jonathan, will be the youngest person by many years ever to have won it."

Sir Hartley stopped talking and a curious silence followed. Jonathan broke it. "They killed Henry Wright," he blurted out.

It was Sir Hartley's turn to be surprised. "Is that true?" he asked, and the others nodded their confirmation.

Sir Hartley walked to the window and studied the sunlit scene outside. Jonathan watched him and saw his shoulders sag for a little while and then come back straight again like a soldier on parade. When Sir Hartley turned to face them the smile had gone and it was hard to say what expression had taken its place. Resignation perhaps. And with it strength.

When he spoke, the words came softly. "In events like this there are winners and losers," he said. "Poor Henry was a loser."